GHOSTS OF
NORTH
CENTRAL INDIANA

GHOSTS OF NORTH CENTRAL INDIANA

DOROTHY SALVO BENSON AND W.C. MADDEN

Haunted America

Published by Haunted America
A Division of The History Press
Charleston, SC
www.historypress.com

Front cover: The Monroe Seiberling Mansion in Kokomo, Indiana. *W.C. Madden photo.*

First published 2022

Manufactured in the United States

ISBN 9781467151054

Library of Congress Control Number: 2022937892

Notice: The information in this book is true and complete to the best of our knowledge. It is offered without guarantee on the part of the authors or The History Press. The authors and The History Press disclaim all liability in connection with the use of this book.

This book is dedicated to all who trusted in me to share their personal stories. To my family, for encouraging me and giving support. To my husband, Matthew. With him I have found meaningful love, balance and a positive core. To my children, for whom my pride and love are endless.
—Dorothy Salvo Benson

This book is dedicated to my wife, who stands by me and makes me a better person and writer as she edits all of my work to make it much better, including this book.
—W.C. Madden

CONTENTS

CONTENTS

ACKNOWLEDGEMENTS

Thank you to those who were willing to share their personal experiences and encounters to make this book happen. To the businesses and public locations who took the time to speak with us and let us explore, we appreciate you sharing your time and information. A special acknowledgment to Wolfe's Leisure Time Campground owners Dale and Mary Wolfe for their time, for allowing us to explore the grounds and for providing many generations with the opportunity to make memories at their location.

Introduction

Have you ever been alone in a room and felt someone was watching you? Heard a voice come out of nowhere when nobody was around or caught the image of something out of the corner of your eye? If so, you're not alone, and it could be possible that if you try, you may just tune something in that is not living.

Indiana, affectionately called the Hoosier State by its residents, has a vast history. Folklore and mysteries go back generations, and ghostly encounters are not a rare experience in this state. There have been many over the years who experienced puzzling happenings, leaving them baffled by what they saw. Some dismiss paranormal encounters; others explain them by the use of conventional science. Many allow themselves to accept the explanations given to them as a way to rationalize and not feel crazy. When a person encounters a disembodied voice, a visual apparition or even a moment from another time, it would be easy to say they are experiencing a mental lapse. However, when that experience impacted their life, changing its course—often for the better—is it wrong to believe that the person was helped along by someone or something not of this world?

Journey with us now by reading some of the personal and life-changing paranormal experiences from those who were brave enough to share their encounters. Indiana has had many people over the years who have bled and died making a home on its soils. Others have battled and fought, leaving a part of themselves behind. Even more have raised their families and made memories, calling Indiana their home. In some situations, there have been those who lost their lives unjustly at the hands of another. Their memories and the stories of what befell them need to be imprinted on the state's timeline and remembered. If you do not respect those who came before, you may just find that Indiana's past residents and passersby will come back and make sure you remember them! Let's face it, we will all die, and what happens next is not something anyone can absolutely guarantee. For many, experiencing the paranormal is a validation that life does go on, loved ones still exist and there is a chance you can one day come back, even after death.

This book covers the north-central counties of Indiana, including the counties of Benton, Blackford, Carroll, Clinton, Fountain, Fulton, Grant, Howard, Huntington, Jasper, LaPorte, Miami, Newton, Pulaski, Tippecanoe, Tipton, Wabash, Warren and White. Be sure to check out our related past titles, *Haunted Lafayette* and *Haunted Tales from The Region: Ghosts of Indiana's South Shore*, and keep an eye out for additional titles coming from us.

CHAPTER 1
BENTON COUNTY

SCARY THEATER IN FOWLER

Fowler is a small community located thirty miles west of Purdue University in West Lafayette. This Benton County town might be small, but people travel to the area from everywhere, drawn in by the ghostly apparitions said to be seen at the old movie theater.

Located at 111 East Fifth Street, the movie theater was originally built in 1940, so it's designed in the Art Deco style. Over time, the theater began to slowly give in to age and disrepair, until new life was brought into the building during renovation. Today, the marquee shines as brightly as ever, but the renovations seem to have stirred up paranormal activity.

Numerous thrill seekers and paranormal investigation groups have explored the theater and come back with their own personal encounters and eyewitness accounts of apparitions. EVPs (electronic voice phenomena), disembodied voices and strange sounds have all been reported. The question at this location is not *if* you will have a paranormal encounter but instead, what kind of encounter will you have?

Linda is a self-confessed thrill seeker, and after getting off her shift waiting tables one evening, she convinced her coworkers to take an adventure with her. She had it in her mind that they would go by the Fowler Theater in the early morning hours and see what all the talk was about. She admits that to many, her claiming to have a paranormal experience would be tossed aside as something questionable.

The waitress said her previous experiences looking into the paranormal are well known by her friends and family. She feels they doubt her; they have told her they think she perceives the encounters because she has adrenaline pumping and is anticipating she will bump into a ghost. "Actually, that is probably true in most cases. After I get home, I calm down," Linda explained. "I realize the quick glimpse of what I thought I saw could have been passing headlights. Still, I have never seen a full-bodied apparition before I was outside the theater like I did the night I am talking about."

Linda and her two friends arrived at the Fowler Theater just after two in the morning and parked their car. The small group stood outside and called out to the spirit world to show itself. Having a laugh, they spent the next twenty minutes or so daring anything not of this world to make its presence known. Linda admitted it was immature, but at the time, she thought of it as harmless fun; they were just trying to scare themselves. Finally, Linda's two friends walked back to the car, and Linda said she would be there as soon as she finished her smoke.

This is when Linda had a life-changing experience that altered the way she viewed the paranormal. As Linda was about to turn and head toward the others, she heard the sound of a child giggling. She looked all around her but saw no one. At this point, she told herself it was the wind and she was jumpy from their earlier fun. Taking her first step to walk away, she was stunned when a little boy suddenly ran past her.

> It happened so fast! He was like a blur as he ran by, and the only thing I could distinguish was that his hair was black and he was the height of maybe an eight-year-old. As he went past me, I was hit with an icy cold breeze and in that brief moment, I don't think I thought he was a ghost, but this kid was illogically outside running down the sidewalk in the middle of the night. It was when I turned around to see where he was running that I almost fell over. He ran right toward where the others stood by the car and dissolved into thin air!

Linda took a deep breath as she thought back to the encounter. She took a minute trying to bring herself under control as she further shared her experience. Outside the theater, she felt frozen in place. When she finally found her voice, she started to scream, and the others rushed over to her. She was frustrated when they told her they had seen nobody, even though they had been watching her the whole time. Linda admitted she was shaken by this experience for a long time and did not explore the supernatural for a while. Now she has gone back to exploring the paranormal, but she revealed she does it with a higher level of respect and awareness. "As humans, we have no real control over how the things we are trying to learn will respond to us" a wiser Linda shared.

CHAPTER 2
BLACKFORD COUNTY

BLOOD ROAD HAUNTED

Blood Road in Dunkirk was named as such for good reason, according to the Will County Ghost Hunters Society (theghostpage.com). Local legend has it that a father was upset with his son and tied him to the back of his truck, dragging him to his death. People have reported seeing a large section of the road was bloodstained, but when they looked again, it was gone.

The apparition of the small boy has been seen walking along the very stretch of road that he was killed on. Blood Road is actually County Road 700. The town is located in both Blackford and Jay Counties. It was originally called Quincy.

CHAPTER 3
CARROLL COUNTY

GHOSTS BY ADAMS MILL BRIDGE

The Adams Mill Covered Bridge is an old wooden bridge located where Adams Mill Road meets Roop's Mill Road near the town of Cutler. It spans the Little Pipe Creek.

A legend has it that if you drive past the mill across the bridge, stop and get out of your car, you will be able to see several apparitions walking near the river, according to the Will County Ghost Hunters Society. If the figures are approached, they will disappear into thin air.

Another tale has it that people have used the bridge to get rid of babies born out of wedlock. Although the local, county-maintained bridge seems

The Adams Mill Bridge was first built in 1872, so it's been around a long time. *W.C. Madden photo.*

tranquil during the day, the night brings about another situation, according to a 2012 article in *Carroll County Magazine*.

The magazine also explained there is a crybaby bridge somewhere in Carroll County. According to numerous stories, many people have had strange encounters at the bridge with children long dead. They have heard the cries of a baby that was tossed from the bridge. One far-fetched story has it that a slave owner got a slave girl pregnant and dumped her baby over the bridge.

THE DELPHI MURDERS

This sign marks the Monon High Bridge Trail, and items have been left at its base to honor the murder victims. *W.C. Madden photo.*

Back on February 14, 2017, the bodies of Abigail "Abby" Williams and Liberty "Libby" German were discovered on a hiking trail in Delphi. The two had disappeared from the trail the previous day. Abby was thirteen, and her friend Libby was fourteen.

The Indiana State Police and the FBI were called in to assist the Carroll County Sheriff's Department and the Delphi Police Department with the murders. More than twenty-five thousand tips later, the suspected murderer is still at large.

Several people have held spirit and ghost box sessions trying to solve the murder mystery but with no success. Ghost hunters have recorded some EVPs at the Monon High Bridge, where a video of the murder suspect was captured on Libby's cellphone. An eerie animated video was also produced by Investigator Gray Hughes to show the walk cycle of the murder suspect.

The county has blocked that portion of the trail to prevent people from using it any longer; however, curious visitors can simply walk around the barricade.

Anyone with information regarding this crime is encouraged to contact law enforcement by utilizing the tip hotline: abbyandlibbytip@cacoshrf.com or (765) 822-3535 (Indiana State Police).

CHAPTER 4

CASS COUNTY

THE GHOST IN THE ROAD

In 1977, Dan P. of Logansport was on his way to his girlfriend's parents' home in Monticello. The time was around nine in the evening, and the weather outside was cold and dark. He was running late and excited to see his girl, as it had been over a week since he last saw her.

While listening to music and not minding the road ahead, Dan nearly hit a man who appeared in the middle of the road on U.S. 24. He swerved and nearly lost control of his car. He was shaken, so he pulled the car over to the side of the road and got out. The culprit of his near accident was still in the road, continuing his walk in the opposite direction.

Dan was annoyed and screamed at the man, "What is wrong with you! Get out of the road!"

The man turned and looked at him. Dan noticed what looked like blood on his clothes and face. The man was a mess and not dressed for the weather. Dan took pity on him and asked, "You need a ride?"

With a rough voice, the man said, "I need to get back to Idaville." He began to walk toward Dan but vanished before he got to the car.

Not sure what to do next, Dan walked in a complete circle around the area, looking for the man. He even walked to the spot where the man had been to see if he had fallen in a hole. He was at a loss. He began to wonder if he had driven off the road and had some sort of dream.

Dan got to his girlfriend's parents' home that night and related his story to his girlfriend. He knew she didn't believe him. In fact, he felt as though his girlfriend thought he was making a creative excuse for once again showing up late.

Still, he found himself looking in the paper over the next couple of weeks to see if anyone had turned up missing.

A person's future becomes his past through the present. That night, Dan's run off the road had branded itself past, present, and future. It will forever remind him that all things are possible.

STRANGER ON THE TRAIL

On a mid-July day, while vacationing in Cass County, Rob and Lisa P. decided to enjoy a nature hike at France Park, located on U.S. 24 near Logansport. The sun was beginning to set. The day had been warm, and the cool breeze that came with dusk felt great to them.

They were camping and enjoying their much-needed vacation. Rob was a broker in downtown Chicago, and Lisa was a paralegal. With such stressful jobs, they enjoyed their summer retreat each year to Indiana Beach and the surrounding area. This vacation, like previous ones, was going along perfectly—until a stranger appeared on the trail.

"Do you want to stop up ahead and catch our breath?" Rob asked Lisa. He could tell she was tired after hiking a while, but he knew she wouldn't confess to it.

"Sure, we can rest if you want," Lisa replied, shrugging. She was relieved when she was able to put the backpack she had been carrying on the ground.

"This is beautiful!" Rob exclaimed, as he looked at the view in front of him. On a rock cliff up above the lake, the setting sun created a masterpiece. France Park was once a rock quarry.

Rob was brought back from his state of peace by the sound of whistling. Disappointed at being interrupted, he asked, "Lisa, do you hear that?"

France Park is located on U.S. 24 not far from Logansport. *W.C. Madden photo.*

Lisa heard the whistling as well and knew someone was coming in their direction. "It's just someone hiking," she said. "They'll just pass by."

Lisa looked back to the view before her. The shuffling of feet sounded closer now. Rob turned his head to nod a hello to the hiker as a young man in his late teens appeared. He was wearing outdated swim trunks that seemed to be wet, and his shaggy hair was plastered to his head. When he saw the couple, he stopped and smiled.

"That is not a safe place to sit," the teen said, with a matter-of-fact attitude. He seemed full of confidence and a bit mischievous.

"Hey, kid. It looks like you need to take your own advice; looks as if you have fallen in yourself!" Rob retorted with annoyance.

Lisa thought Rob's response was a little harsh, but she remained quiet.

Rob readied himself for a smart comeback, but the teen just smiled and began to whistle again.

"Just ignore him," said Lisa.

Rob looked in Lisa's direction and saw the pleading in her eyes, so he turned to tell the teen to be on his way.

Both of them were surprised when they could still hear the whistling in front of them, but the teen had disappeared. The sound of shuffling feet and whistling moved further down the path until it could no longer be heard, but neither could see the teen. He had vanished before their very eyes.

After a few years, the couple returned to France Park again, despite their encounter with the mysterious teen. They both admit to having been frightened in the moment but say that their experience reminded them that things happen that cannot be explained.

"How boring this life would be if we knew all its secrets," Rob explained.

MOUNT HOPE CEMETERY

The third-largest cemetery in Indiana, Mount Hope, may just be haunted, according to a number of sources. Mount Hope is located in Logansport. It is some two hundred acres and includes the Ninth Street Cemetery, which began in 1828. Mount Hope began in 1854.

Supposedly, if you go just after midnight and the conditions are just right, you can hear the sound of galloping horses. Standing in a particular part of the cemetery grounds, when the wind is still, you can hear an eerie whistling, the sound of cannon fire next to the war memorial and the sound

This war memorial in Mount Hope Cemetery is where you supposedly can still hear the sound of cannon fire. *W.C. Madden photo.*

of whistles. The war memorial recognizes all from the county who died in the Revolutionary War up to the Spanish-American War.

Also, an inscription on a mausoleum is somewhat intriguing. It says, "Knock three times and they shall come." Who are they?

SHILOH CHURCH HAS GHOSTS

The Shiloh Christian Church in rural Logansport has had numerous paranormal events, according to the Will County Ghost Hunters Society.

Legend says that on nights with a full moon, a headless horseman will appear at midnight. If you walk around the church three times at night, then look into a basement window, the apparition of a little girl will be staring back at you. A mysterious semitruck will appear out of nowhere and chase people, too.

The church also has a creepy-looking cemetery nearby.

The Shiloh Christian Church is located in a rural area northwest of Logansport. *W.C. Madden photo.*

CHAPTER 5
CLINTON COUNTY

HAUNTED HAMILTON ROAD

Founded in 1858 and located in Clinton County, Mulberry is a small town that has an old-world charm reminiscent of days gone by. The city park is well maintained, and homeowners keep their yards nicely landscaped in the summer months, finishing off the picturesque appeal.

Despite the welcoming atmosphere of the town, it is known for having one of the most haunted stretches of road in Indiana: Hamilton Road. Some of the claims fit classic ghost story stereotypes. They include a haunted bridge where, if you flash your lights three times, you will be met with an apparition who gives chase. Other claims are of the sudden appearance of a ghostly train steaming down the tracks.

Of course, you can't hold the title of being one of the most eerie roads in a state without the claim of an apparition that suddenly appears in drivers' back seats or of the hitchhiker who disappears shortly after being picked up. In the case of Hamilton Road, the disappearing spirit is not that of a beautiful young girl; instead, witnesses describe a short, stout young man who suddenly becomes angry before disappearing.

If you talk to Ryan, who drove Hamilton Road for years when he was working for a meat supplier, he will share with you about a ghostly cat he believes haunts the road. He first encountered the skinny gray/black cat on an early winter morning. As he was driving down Hamilton Road, he suddenly heard meowing inside of his truck.

This is the haunted bridge on Hamilton Road, located near Mulberry. *W.C. Madden photo.*

Ryan was startled when a cat appeared on the passenger seat beside him. He pulled over, trying to search his mind for when the cat could have gotten inside his truck. Ryan opened the door and put the cat outside his employer's truck, despite it being winter temperatures outside.

The situation struck Ryan as odd, but he did not give it much thought; he certainly didn't think it was within the realm of the paranormal. He told his wife about it later that night. She scolded him for leaving the cat in the cold. He assured her that he also was feeling guilty and if he ever found another cat in his truck, he would bring it home.

In truth, he never expected to come across the cat again, but that is exactly what happened when he was passing the same stretch of highway almost three weeks later at the same time of day. He described the cat's sudden appearance once again as an exact replica of the first time. Now he was really perplexed and struggled to try to imagine at what point the cat got into his truck.

Despite his confusion, he recalled the promise he made to his wife and this time kept driving, deciding to take the cat home. He changed his route, deciding to make a quick stop at his home to leave the cat with his wife. He admits the cat was rough-looking; she was thin and missing some patches of hair.

The cat's appearance aside, she was very good-natured and jumped onto Ryan's lap for a few moments, purring while she was patted, before returning to the passenger seat, where she curled up comfortably in the warmth of the truck and seemed to fall asleep.

Ryan pulled up along the curb outside his home. He left the driver's side and walked around to pick the cat up off the passenger seat of his truck. When he opened the door, the cat was gone! He searched everywhere inside the truck and outside, unable to find where the cat had disappeared to.

Desperate to solve the mystery, he even rolled under the truck to see if the cat had been climbing underneath to catch a ride. His wife came out and was startled by how passionate Ryan was in trying to convince her and himself the cat was right there. The experience greatly frustrated him, but he was still not having any notions of it being a ghostly situation on his radar.

By early the following fall, Ryan had all but forgotten about the cat and was driving his normal route down North Hamilton Road in the early morning when he suddenly heard the familiar cat's meow once again. He jumped at the sound but kept his pace along the road, looking over, expecting to see the cat make an appearance. The meowing continued to sound from within the truck, but the cat did not show itself.

Ryan found a place to pull over, and as soon as he did, the cat appeared on his passenger side floor. Ryan was reaching for the cat while he racked his brain, trying to make sense of the cat reappearing—when his hands passed through the animal, and it was gone! Ryan jumped back in his seat, paralyzed with the sudden awareness that the cat was an apparition.

Ryan was greatly unnerved by his experience and still struggles to admit to anyone, let alone himself, that he was witness to a paranormal occurrence. He knows for certain the cat was there, and then suddenly it was not, and if that fits the definition of a paranormal occurrence, then he accepts that. What he did not accept was continuing to drive that route. The day following his last encounter with the cat, he insisted to his employer that he needed to change routes.

Ryan can't explain what happened to him. Since then, he has heard of similar ghostly claims along Hamilton Road in Mulberry. Despite his own experience, he still struggles to believe some of the claims are not exaggerated but does admit there is something unusual about that stretch of highway where the unexplained happens.

Hamilton Road is a dangerous route to take in the winter months and is known for accidents. There are claims that there was a church that burned down in the 1800s, but there is no record of this to be found. Whoever or whatever haunts Hamilton Road may never be identified, but it is wise to slow down and drive carefully as you pass, just in case you're suddenly startled by a cat or something else.

CHAPTER 6
FOUNTAIN COUNTY

HAUNTED WABASH SHORE APARTMENTS

Carol was a forty-something recently divorced woman trying to mend a broken heart when she moved to Covington from Danville to stay with her cousin while she got back on her feet. She thought she had found a new community to call home. Carol's cousin lived at the Wabash Shore Apartments in Covington. The place was clean and had a welcoming atmosphere. Carol immediately loved the Covington community, describing it as picturesque and the people as friendly.

Carol settled in and found herself a job at a factory nearby. She began to make friends and become familiar with the area, thinking more and more how this was the place that was going to be her new home. Carol had never had a paranormal experience, and when she encountered her first "odd" event, a ghostly happening never occurred to her. She was sleeping when, at about three in the morning, she awoke to the smell of rubbing alcohol. The scent was strong, and she got up to search for the source. She could not determine where the odor was coming from, as everything appeared normal. It was a very comfortable early summer day, so the heat was not on, nor was the air conditioner running.

Carol lay back down to fall asleep again when she heard the sound of someone exhaling. She sat straight up, looked around again and saw nothing, deciding it was her imagination. The next morning, she asked her cousin about the odor, but her cousin had no idea what Carol was talking about. For the next couple of weeks, every night at about the same time, the odor reappeared. Carol even tried waking her cousin to smell what she was talking about, but each time, the smell suddenly vanished. She gave up and decided to ignore it.

About a month after the smell first started, Carol woke one night to the sound of cabinets closing. She walked into the kitchen, and all the cabinets were wide open. This startled her. She was the only one in the apartment, as her cousin had left for the weekend to visit other family members. Carol immediately regretted staying behind, and for the first time in her life, she began to wonder about the possibility of a ghost. Her hands shaking, she closed all the cabinets and turned on all the lights before going back to bed.

Carol was just about to doze off when she heard a whisper in her ear. The voice said, "I am here." The voice was clear, but Carol could not distinguish whether it was male or female. Carol was paralyzed with fear; she squeezed the blanket around her, closed her eyes as tight as she could and was unable to move. That night, she lay still, her heart pounding. At some point, she drifted off to sleep, waking only to wonder if she had imagined the whole thing.

After showering the next morning, Carol was getting dressed when she heard noise coming from the kitchen. She wondered if her cousin had returned a little earlier than expected, so she called out her cousin's name and got no response. As she was about to walk toward the kitchen, she heard a door slam. She ran to the main entrance and found the door swinging wide open. She felt this was very odd, because she had just heard it slamming shut. Stepping into the kitchen, she found things knocked over on the counter and cabinets wide open; it looked like the kitchen had been rifled through. She worried someone had been there trying to rob them and she had interrupted them by calling out to her cousin.

Carol stepped outside and saw nobody. There were a couple of kids playing outside, and she asked them if they had seen anyone come out of her apartment. They had not noticed anyone, and an older woman walking her dog shared the same feedback. No one had witnessed anyone coming from the apartment. Who, then, had made all the noise and caused the mess in the kitchen? Who had left the front door wide open? This was the last straw. Carol was concerned. Either she going through something that was not of this world, or she was losing her mind. She had to talk to someone about what was happening and find some sense of realistic possibilities.

Carol talked to her cousin about what had happened when she returned from her visit with family. Her cousin suggested to her that maybe she was having a mental breakdown as a result of her divorce. Carol rationalized to herself that she had been feeling unusually calm and happy for someone just leaving a twenty-one-year marriage. She began to wonder if she was suppressing some emotions and this was leading to her imagining things. Carol called a few therapists and, settling on one, scheduled an appointment for two weeks out. The next evening, she had a friend come over after work to binge-watch her favorite show, *The Big Bang Theory*. She felt it was time to focus on the future and engage in healthy activities like spending time with friends and not so much time alone.

Carol was feeling good and having a nice visit; she had completely taken her mind off the strange happenings. She had convinced herself she had imagined the whole thing. Excusing herself to use the bathroom, Carol smiled to herself about how silly she had been over the last month, being scared of her own shadow. She reached out to pull open the bathroom door when she caught a quick glimpse of a long-sleeved arm reaching from the other side and pulling it closed. Suddenly, the smell of rubbing alcohol filled her nostrils, and she screamed as she turned to run. Before she could even worry about what her friend would think, she realized her friend was moving fast to the outside door.

Once outside, both women took deep, calming breaths, needing to compose themselves before talking. To Carol's surprise, her friend immediately told Carol the apartment was haunted. Carol had told her nothing about her prior experiences. This was a shock to Carol, while also making her feel validated that she had not been crazy or having a mental breakdown all along. Her friend told Carol that as soon as Carol walked away to use the bathroom, she smelled rubbing alcohol, and then someone whispered in her ear, "I am here." That was all Carol needed to hear. She packed up, thanked her cousin for allowing her to stay and moved back to Danville to live with the friend who had shared her paranormal experience.

Carol made a point of emphasizing that her cousin never experienced anything unusual in the apartment the entire time she lived there. This has made Carol wonder if she has the ability to tune into things some people cannot. Even if this is the case, Carol shared that she has not developed any interest in exploring the paranormal and, in fact, usually avoids the subject whenever it comes up, for fear of someone whispering in her ear once again.

CHAPTER 7
FULTON COUNTY

MONSTER IN LAKE MANITOU

In 1838, an article was published in the *Logansport Telegraph* describing a "monster" in Lake Manitou measuring about sixty feet long.

It had a long, muscular body with what looked like a cow's head (only much, much larger). The Potawatomi word Manitou translates to both "good spirit" and "evil spirit," so it's understandable that folks might have been a bit leery of it. Sightings and rumors have persisted over the decades, and to this day, some people still swear they saw the bizarre, yellow-splotched monster lurking in the depths.

This story is a lot like that of the Loch Ness monster in Scotland. Popular interest and belief in the creature there brought worldwide attention in 1933. Evidence of its existence is anecdotal, including a hoax photograph and sonar readings.

CEMETERY HAUNTED BY BOY

A cemetery in Rochester is haunted by a boy, according to the Will County Ghost Hunters Society.

The cemetery is haunted by a three-year-old boy named Earl. The boy has been seen playing near the tree by his grave. People have also heard his disembodied voice.

The cemetery is located just off State Road 25 on 300 South.

OLD SLAUGHTERHOUSE REAPPEARS

An old slaughterhouse on Olson Road in Rochester has been reported as being seen, according to the Will County Ghost Hunters Society.

The slaughterhouse is now gone, but people have said that on occasion they can see it, and then it disappears into thin air. It was located on Olson Road between the old and new U.S. 31.

HAUNTED SCHOOL

The Prill School Museum in Akron is haunted, according to the Will County Ghost Hunters Society. It was located in Henry Township District No. 3.

A former teacher named Sister Sarah has been seen around the school, most often beside a large tree in the schoolyard. People have said they can hear children laughing and playing at all hours of the day and night. A grave belonging to one of Sister Sarah's babies was located underneath the first step leading into the school.

Built in 1876, the school closed in 1925. Local citizens restored it in 1971 and got it listed on the National Register of Historic Places in 1981. The school is now a historic one-room museum.

The Prill Museum School is haunted by a former teacher and children. *W.C. Madden photo.*

CHAPTER 8
GRANT COUNTY

JAMES DEAN'S GRAVE HAUNTED

Fairmount is famous for the being the hometown of actor James Dean, who appeared in several movies. Dean is buried in Park Cemetery, and people have reported feeling a very strong, overpowering presence when visiting there, according to the Will County Ghost Hunters Society. Some people swear they have been touched by unseen hands.

The Academy Award winner died on September 30, 1955. He was driving a Porsche on his way to a road race when he slammed into a 1950 Ford Tudor and died as a result of his injuries. He was twenty-four.

James Dean's grave is adorned with many items left by visitors, including kisses on his headstone. *W.C. Madden photo.*

HAUNTED BRIDGE

The Tenth Street Bridge in Gas City is haunted, according to the Will County Ghost Hunters Society.

During construction of the bridge back in the early 1900s, a construction worker fell off the bridge and died. People have reported seeing the apparition of the man clinging to the side of the bridge. Some have even heard the man's screams.

OLD EAST SCHOOL HAUNTED

The Old East School is haunted, according to the Will County Ghost Hunters Society. People have reported hearing the laughter of children and seeing the merry-go-round spinning around by itself in the playground behind the elementary school.

The school was first built in 1894 in the Romanesque style. The building was listed on the National Register of Historic Places on March 5, 2004. Then the old school was rehabbed in 2005 by the Gas City Historical Society to house senior citizens. It is now called the Gas City School Apartments.

CHARLES ROAD MURDER

A family murder on Charles Road near Marion is responsible for hauntings there, according to the Will County Ghost Hunters Society.

During the early 1900s, a family was headed down Charles Road one winter evening in their wagon on their way to church. The family never arrived at church, causing their fellow church members to go looking for them. The family's wagon was found on the side of the road, abandoned. The search party found the family in the nearby woods, and they all were brutally murdered. They were all decapitated.

People have reported hearing screams and cries coming from the woods. Several bright white orbs have been seen in the woods, too.

A car passes over the Tenth Street Bridge in Gas City. *W.C. Madden photo.*

The Old East School is now called the Gas City School Apartments. *W.C. Madden photo.*

GHOST AT THE HOSTESS HOUSE

The Wilson-Vaughan Hostess House in Marion is haunted by a woman who was murdered there many years ago, according to the Will County Ghost Hunters Society.

Jessie Saul had been a receptionist and live-in manager in the four-story mansion for a decade when she met her fate. Joseph Allen Sandoval, who was out celebrating his twenty-first birthday at a local topless bar, broke in and sexually molested Saul. Then he brutally bashed her head in. Police found blood splattered all over the bedroom and Saul's dead body at the foot of the bed. It was one of the most brutal murders in Marion's history. Sandoval was later arrested, tried and convicted of murder. He was given forty years in prison.

The woman's apparition has been seen wearing a long white gown in the mansion and on the balcony.

The mansion was built in 1912 as a wedding gift from J. Wood Wilson to his wife, Lillian Pampel. It's now a place for weddings and other social events, and lunch is served on weekdays. You can tour the historic landmark on weekdays, too.

The Hostess House is haunted by the apparition of a woman killed there. *W.C. Madden photo.*

SPOOK'S CORNER

Spook's Corner in Upland is where a school bus supposedly went off the road and several children were killed, according to the Will County Ghost Hunters Society.

The apparitions of these young children have been seen many times. The sounds of children screaming, crying and yelling for help can also be heard coming from this area.

MISSISSINEWA GRAVEYARD IS HAUNTED

A dozen tombstones at the Mississinewa Battle Grounds Cemetery mark the graves of the members of Lieutenant Colonel John B. Campbell's command who lost their lives in the Battle of Mississinewa on December 17–18, 1812. The battle occurred during the War of 1812, between American troops and the Miami tribe. General William Henry Harrison ordered an attack on Miami Indian villages in response to attacks on Fort Wayne and Fort Harrison. Campbell led a force of six hundred mounted troops and attacked two Miami villages along the Mississinewa River, killing a large number of Indians and capturing seventy-six prisoners, including thirty-four women and children.

In the cemetery near Marion, people have encountered apparitions, strange flashes of light and shadowy figures. One of the headstones supposedly has had blood flow from it. Sounds of disembodied moans, voices and strange noises are heard in the graveyard and the surrounding woods. People have seen the apparitions of Indians running through the woods and witnessed the historic phantoms of U.S. troops marching through the fields.

CHAPTER 9
HOWARD COUNTY

OLD JACOB'S FUNERAL HOME WAS HAUNTED

The Old Jacob's Funeral Home in Kokomo was haunted, according to several sources. The funeral home became the House of Jordan Entertainment, but back in the early 1900s, the building was the only Black-owned funeral home in central Indiana.

Built in 1901, the home has an eerie look. People have reported seeing shadows, apparitions, orbs, ectoplasmic mist and other things. There have been numerous electrical disturbances, disembodied voices, footsteps and knocking, too. Most activity occurs in the basement.

The current owner, who wishes to remain anonymous, purchased the building in 2000. He admitted he has seen black shadowy figures on several occasions, but he doesn't believe in ghosts. He said previous workers and renters in the building heard sounds and saw shadows during all hours. He said that children have seen a "black fog" in different rooms during the night. He also said there are whispers in the hallways and lights go on and off. Workers during the remodeling reported a high-pitched drilling noise coming from the basement.

The owner called a psychic, who told him the remodeling was stirring up the spirits in the building. "You, sir, are playing with fire," she said.

The owner also consulted with a local Christian pastor, who came over and sprinkled holy water around the home. After the pastor left, things went wrong again. Lights would turn on and off, and the owner would get

The House of Jordan is now the headquarters for the Howard County Republican Party. *W.C. Madden photo.*

lightheaded sometimes. His wife doesn't want to be alone when she's in the building. They hoped to get rid of some of the things in the funeral home by selling them on eBay. Their intention was to remove anything that may have a ghostly connection to it, stimulating paranormal disturbances.

The building is located on the 1300 block of South Main Street, on the west side of the street.

ARMSTRONG STREET HOUSE HAUNTED

A house on Armstrong Street in Kokomo was haunted and appeared on Syfy's *Paranormal Witness*.

Ann and Roger Brock moved into a small home at 2220 North Armstrong Street in Kokomo in 1970 with their twin daughters, Lana and Lisa, and another daughter, Mary, according to the website Haunted Places.

Lana began hearing clicking and clawing noises on the ceiling, attic and walls. She complained to her mother, who thought she just had a good imagination.

When she became a teen, she saw apparitions in the back bedroom. Then she saw what looked like a man outside with his face pressed up against the window. The police were called, but nothing came of it.

Lana and her siblings also saw a solid, dark mass that would hover above them in bed. In 1981, during a garage sale, they found out from a woman that her sister had been murdered in the back room.

In 1983, the family had company come over, and Roger slept on the floor in the living room. He was awakened by something scratching his leg. Ann described it as a green leprechaun.

The family had a Baptist pastor come over to the house to bless it. However, the activity only escalated. They started hearing louder noises, and furniture would move.

One day, when the family returned from church, they couldn't get in the front door. They were able to unlock the door, but the door wouldn't budge. Finally, they broke a window to get in. They found the bookcase had been moved to block the door, and books were scattered around the room.

Another incident occurred later. Roger was sitting in the kitchen studying the Bible when the ceiling fell in on him. He wasn't hurt, but he knew something wasn't right. Many other incidents occurred while the family was there.

In 2001, the house was burned down by a serial arsonist, and the lot has remained empty ever since.

Roger passed away in 2005, and Lana became a paranormal investigator.

TWO OLD HISTORIC BUILDINGS HAUNTED

The Howard County Historical Society has two buildings that are supposedly haunted.

The Monroe Seiberling Mansion has long been known for ghost sightings, according to the website Haunted Places of Indiana. The mansion was first built in the late 1880s and first revealed in March 1890 when a surrounding structure was taken down. It has gone through a number of owners and is now the Howard County Museum. People who have gone on tours there have stated they have seen many ghosts in the huge building. One sighting was of a woman sitting in a rocking chair in one of the rooms upstairs.

Next door to the Seiberling Mansion is the Elliott House, which is also run by the society. Built in 1889, the house was named after its second owner,

The Elliott House is located at 1215 West Sycamore Street. *W.C. Madden photo.*

Matthew Elliott. In 1930, the Harvey family moved into the house. During the five years the family lived there, their five-year-old son fell from a second-story window and died. The spirit of the Harvey boy is still alive in the house. He's been heard upstairs, near the window he fell from, according to the website the Kokomo Post. And he's been seen outside.

THE ORIGINAL TREASURE MART HAUNTED

The Original Treasure Mart on East Vaile Street is haunted, according to the Kokomo Post.

The Indiana Ghost Trackers have gone in the old building and found it haunted. While the investigators were attempting to communicate with a spirit, it turned the security lights on and off. The investigators and others have seen a little girl walking around the store and looking around. Her apparition has also been seen in the shop. "They heard a child laughing," said Diane Amburgey, a clerk at the store.

The Original Treasure Mart was built in 1887 and is haunted. *W.C. Madden photo.*

Diane said the old building was constructed in 1887 and was once used to house World War II prisoners of war. It also had a tunnel that led to another building. She said the group asked the ghosts if they were Germans, and they replied, "No, we're Italian."

The group went downstairs to the basement, and all the lights were out. They asked if someone was down there, and the lights came back on, Diane explained.

A vendor upstairs claimed that their toys were moved one night, Amburgey said.

Another gentleman said he once smelled cigar smoke in the place, but no smoking is allowed.

HOUSE HAUNTED BY ELDERLY LADY

At the intersection of Carter Road and 400 North outside Kokomo, an old house sits on the northeast corner and is haunted by an elderly lady, according to the Will County Ghost Hunters Society.

A man lived with this lady in the home until she passed away. Shortly after her death, the man began seeing apparitions, hearing footsteps and experiencing electrical disturbances. He couldn't deal with the activity and moved out. People have seen apparitions and bright glowing orbs moving past the windows and around the home.

SATAN CHURCH

An old boarded-up church located in the country near Russiaville is well known to be haunted, according to the Will County Ghost Hunters Society.

A graveyard there is said to have been used by cults to perform rituals. People have reported seeing red glowing eyes in the church and among the tombstones. People have also reported seeing glowing orbs and a heavy mist. Disembodied voices, whispers, and growling noises have also been reported. The activity takes place in the church as well as the graveyard.

APARTMENTS ARE CURSED

The Garden Square apartment complex in Kokomo has an eerie look about it and is said to be cursed.

The Garden Square apartment complex was built on top of a cemetery. *W.C. Madden photo.*

People have reported seeing apparitions, including a pair of legs, moving shadows and what appears to be teardrops and blood dripping from the ceiling. Also, doors opening and closing as well as electrical appliances turning on and off by themselves have been reported. An unseen force has levitated infants, children and pets. Many people believe the place is evil and refuse to ever go back.

JEROME CEMETERY HAUNTED

Jerome is a small unincorporated community near Kokomo with an old cemetery that is supposedly haunted, according to many sources.

People have reported seeing a man dressed in all black, wearing a cape, with two large black dogs with glowing red eyes walking around Jerome Cemetery in Jerome, according to the Will County Ghost Hunters Society. Several people have reported being chased out of the cemetery by the man and the dogs. One person who lives by the cemetery claims to have seen many things. Once he looked out his bedroom window and saw his yard, the trees and even his mailbox covered with ectoplasm.

The Jerome Cemetery began in 1846. *W.C. Madden photo.*

Even the town has some ghost stories. A dilapidated building, which dates back to the 1920s and the days of Prohibition, was haunted.

More about the cemetery can be found in the books *Indiana's Jerome Cemetery and the Hound of Hell* and *Weird Indiana*.

CHAPTER 10

JASPER COUNTY

THE GHOSTS OF ST. JOSEPH'S COLLEGE

St. Joseph's College was founded in 1889 and closed down in 2017, but it has left behind some ghosts. The chapel is one of the oldest buildings on the grounds, and an unknown spirit is located there. A rumored exorcism was conducted at Aquinas Hall. Witnesses have heard voices inside Drexel Hall. Also, Dwenger Hall is rumored to be possessed, and the ghost of a baby is said to haunt Hallas Hall. In the theater building, legend has it that several campus priests hanged themselves after a botched exorcism.

A building on the western edge of campus was originally opened as Troy Hospital in 1869. Nurse Betsy from that hospital, which operated for forty-five years, still inhabits the building today. Reports of moaning or wailing have been reported, as well as the smell of someone baking cookies. Supposedly, Nurse Betsy perished in a fire that took place in the hospital.

HAUNTED STATUE AT MEMORY GARDENS

Locals claim a statue is haunted in Memory Gardens, a cemetery in Rensselaer. The St. Matthew statue at the back of the graveyard is rumored to move at night, keeping watch on visitors. Some say its head and arms will change position.

Left: The chapel at St. Joseph's College has been vacant since the college closed in 2017. It's haunted by an unknown spirit. *W.C. Madden photo.*

Below: The St. Matthew statue at Memory Gardens is rumored to move at night. *W.C. Madden photo.*

The cemetery is closed after dark, and trespassers will be prosecuted, although you can still drive into the cemetery, and the statue is lit at night. Memory Gardens was chartered in 1961 and is one of the most beautiful cemeteries in Jasper County.

THE GHOSTLY TRUCK STOP AREA IN REMINGTON

Ghostly apparitions and eerie encounters off highways and at truck stops often come up in accounts of haunted places. When paranormal events happen in a location that has a history of unfortunate events, including crime and murder, it really makes you pause and consider that there may be something evil about the place. Too many tragic events in one location can't be simply coincidence, can it?

This could be said of the truck stop off I-65 just outside Remington on U.S. 24. The exit off the highway is between two towns, Wolcott and Remington. These communities can boast great small-town living and family appeal. To anyone stopping at one of the three gas stations or fast-food restaurants located nearby, they may appear safe and no different than any other. Sadly, this respite from the highway has had several tragic situations unfold that led to a loss for many. Deaths as a result of accidents and murders, including a victim of the I-65 Serial Killer, have transpired at the businesses off the highway.

On March 3, 1989, the nude body of Jeanne Gilbert, thirty-four, mother of two, was found in a frozen ditch about two miles north of Indiana State Road 18 on the east side of County Road 150 West in White County. The body was not concealed. She had been working at the Remington Days Inn next to the Petro Truck Stop and Iron Skillet restaurant.

On September 19, 2005, a gunman killed two workers at the Family Express convenience store. Lisa Kendall, twenty-nine, of Rensselaer, and Kendora Furr, thirty-eight, were murdered.

Debbie Holmes passes this section of highway almost every weekday on her commute to and from work. A few years ago, she had an unexplained experience in which she feels apparitions played a part in her avoiding a terrible accident. Holmes was traveling from Logansport toward Goodland on U.S. 24 and had just approached the lights at the Remington exit. There was nothing unusual about the day. It was around six thirty, and she was feeling tired but relaxed and ready to go home to watch her favorite shows after she got the kids settled for the night. The radio was playing, and as usual, she was enjoying her long daily drive as her "me time." She suddenly became very alert as she slowed and came to a stop at the red light. Just a little way up ahead, on the side of the road, she saw what looked like a woman walking with a small child. What grabbed her attention was that the location was a very dangerous place to be walking, and she wondered why they were there.

She moved on when the light turned green and turned her eyes to the road in front of her. Suddenly, she jolted and nearly hit her brakes when the same mother and child were suddenly on her left side now and facing her as she drove by. Even though it was only a split second, Holmes said that time seemed to stand still, and she felt like the woman was compelling her in some way to stop. Hands shaking, and not sure why or what exactly had just transpired, Holmes put on her left turn signal and pulled into a McDonald's parking lot.

Just as Holmes pulled into the lot, there was a loud sound as her driver's side tire burst. She did not just have a flat, but the entire tire was shredded, and she was driving on her rim. She was able to come to a safe stop in the nearly empty parking lot. The reality of how dangerous her situation could have been had she stayed on the road, with semitrucks on both sides, made her shudder. She was frustrated but far more relieved than anything else.

After calling for help, Holmes sat and waited. She suddenly remembered the woman and small child she had seen on one side of the road and, a moment later, on the opposite side. Holmes tried to rationalize what she had seen, but it simply was not humanly possible to be on one side of the highway and then on the opposite side in the heavy traffic fifteen seconds later.

Holmes realized that what she saw were apparitions, yet she did not feel afraid. Actually, she began to wonder if they were angels, because had they not appeared, she would not have gotten off the road in the nick of time. Holmes continues to travel the same route Monday through Friday, and despite always keeping an eye out, she has never seen the woman and child she felt saved her life again. In silence, she always sends a mindful thank-you out each time.

Holmes is not the only one to have had a paranormal encounter at the rest stop. Catherine Randall, now retired, worked at the Sunset Inn nearly seventeen years ago. It was during her time there that she became aware there is life after death, and there are things we just do not have any control over. Her first encounter with something ghostly was when she was cleaning one of the rooms in the early morning hours.

Randall had just made up the beds and gone into the bathroom when she heard a loud bang. She jumped and went back into the room to find all the dresser drawers open. This made no sense to her because they had been closed and opening them wouldn't have made a bang.

Randall closed the drawers and carried on despite being puzzled. Nothing happened over the next few weeks, and she had just about forgotten the odd event when another strange occurrence happened.

Randall had just placed her spray bottle of glass cleaner on the sink in the bathroom and bent over to pick up some towels when she heard a whispered voice say, "Looks good." She stood straight up and felt the hair on her arms rise. There was no one else in the room—and certainly no one close enough for her to have heard them whisper clearly. An immediate sensation overcame her, and she felt a presence in the room with her. The air in the room was changing; she described it as feeling cool but having a thickness to it. Her knees felt like Jell-O as she quickly made her way to the outer door of the room. Once outside, she felt lighter and able to breathe deeply. Hands still shaking, she moved on, but she admits she felt her heart race for nearly an hour after the experience.

Not sure herself what happened, Randall did not share her experience with anyone following her second scare. She even felt silly, attempting to rationalize ways her mind could have been playing tricks on her. Despite this, she began to feel unnerved when she was in her own home at night or when she found herself alone.

The cleaning lady believes that during this time, her mind was coming to terms with the fact that there is such a thing as ghosts. This belief in ghosts was driven home when she had her last experience a couple of months later.

Randall was cleaning up a room when a guest knocked on the door, which was already open. He asked her if she had just seen anyone pass by, explaining that someone had been in his room when he was in the bathroom. He told Randall he had the outer door locked, and somehow, someone had come into his room. He went on to say they had opened all his drawers and even opened his suitcase. Nothing was missing, but he felt it to be violating and uncalled-for.

Randall could hear in the guest's voice that he was upset and wanted assistance in the matter. She told him that no one had passed by the room that she had seen. He offended Randall when he commented that she had access to his room and asked if she had gone in for some reason. She began to respond when, to both of their surprise, the drawers in the room directly behind where she was standing flew open. Randall admits she almost ran over the poor man, who stood frozen in place, as she pushed past him, exiting the room.

Stepping into the parking lot, Randall and the guest stared at each other, not sure of what to say. Thinking it was over, Randall was about to ask the guest what he thought had happened when the black, shadowy silhouette of a man came out of the room. He seemed to glide in a mist and entered the room the guest occupied. Randall said she stood in the parking lot with the guest, whom she learned was named Eric, for almost ninety minutes, talking about what they had seen, before he mustered up the courage to run in and grab his suitcase. Eric checked out early, and Randall quit her job immediately and gave no notice. She has no idea what she saw, but it is embedded in her memory. She now knows without any doubt that ghostly entities exist.

A former employee of the Iron Skillet, which was beside the now-closed Sunset Inn, also had paranormal experiences while working there. Wanting to remain anonymous, as he still works in a different part of the truck stop, the man, who we will call Jim, shared his own encounter. The Sunset Inn—once a Holiday Inn and the location of one of the possible victims of the I-65 Serial Killer—has seen several employees come and go over the years. It is not surprising that strange occurrences have been reported at the location.

Jim was walking into work one evening when he saw strange orbs bouncing around the old playground of the Sunset Inn. He watched them for a moment and noticed they seemed to be chasing each other. It was strange, but he did not think much of it at the time. In fact, he even recalled telling himself it must be an optical illusion from the headlights passing by. That was just one of several times he told himself something he saw in that direction was a trick of the lights of passing vehicles.

Once evening, a short time later, Jim went outside to have a smoke. Looking toward the hotel, he saw a tall man walking in his direction at a fast pace. He said the man looked like he was on a mission and had an eerie and ominous look about him. He was white, with dark hair, dressed in jeans and a black shirt. Jim looked away as the man got closer but had an odd feeling and butterflies in his stomach. He began to feel anxious and even fearful. He recalled wondering if this was his sixth sense warning him the man was going to rob the place. He saw the man approach out of the corner of his eye and, on impulse, looked in the man's direction, intending to move out of his way. Jim took a deep nervous breath when he shared what happened next. "I saw him, not even a foot from me, just vanish," he said. "I'm not even joking. He really just disappeared!" Jim recalled the smell of menthol cigarettes that followed the apparition as it disappeared.

Jim knows what he saw and said that the most difficult thing about something like that happening is having no proof to show others you're not crazy. Jim reports strange things still continue to happen at the intersection. He has heard people complain of losing things outside or seeing things that make no sense. He even had a woman come in looking everywhere for her keys, which she said disappeared when she was in the bathroom, only to find them in her car, with the engine running, later. Could this be simple forgetfulness? In Jim's opinion, there is a dark energy that surrounds this area of the Indiana highway. He has not seen any other apparitions but often has felt like he is being watched.

CHAPTER 11

MONTGOMERY COUNTY

HAUNTING AT GENERAL LEW WALLACE LIBRARY

General Lew Wallace, son of Indiana's sixth governor, was a remarkable man in his own right and has gone down in history for writing *Ben Hur*. The accomplished soldier, lawyer, senator and author was a resident of Crawfordsville. His former home no longer stands; however, the study he built for himself remains and is today a museum, preserving his legacy for years to come.

Indianapolis residents John and Carry experienced an eerie occurrence while visiting the museum. The couple was enjoying their tour on a beautiful summer day that was nearing late afternoon. While looking at the artifacts, John occasionally had the impression they were being watched, sending a chill down his back. He quickly dismissed it and focused on the information being presented.

Carry said that toward the end of the tour, she began to feel dizzy and lightheaded, as well as having a sudden stomachache. The feelings were brief and passed in a matter of minutes. She also reported that she felt a presence nearby and experienced the hair on her arms rising, but those feelings ceased when she saw a couple outside the study.

As Carry and John joined hands and began to walk, they suddenly each felt a firm grip on their wrist and hand, and they were torn apart. John described it as an odd and creepy occurrence that he cannot explain. The couple looked around and saw nothing. The summer scenery was beautiful and apparently peaceful.

John tried to lighten the mood and suggested they go get a bite to eat. As they headed toward their car, they very clearly heard a female say, "She's with child." The voice seemed to come from directly beside them, and they both reported having the sensation of someone else there.

At the time, Carry had not even considered she was expecting, as they were not actively trying to have a child. She took a pregnancy test the morning after the strange occurrence and learned she was expecting their first child. The couple has not experienced any paranormal occurrences since the day at the General Lew Wallace Study and Museum. They do not believe they had an encounter with the spirit of Lew Wallace, but they remain curious about who the disembodied female voice belonged to. It did pique their interest in the unknown, and they now explore haunted locations when on vacation.

THE HAUNTED ROTARY JAIL MUSEUM

Many museums today were once homes or establishments rooted in a community's past. It's not surprising to hear of hauntings at these locations, considering the amount of history within. Some jails turned into museums have an especially chilly lore that follows their transformation. What was once a place no one wanted to enter is now a location people pay admission to get into. The Rotary Jail Museum in Crawfordsville is no exception. The museum's webpage states that the rotary jail in Crawfordsville was the first of eighteen rotary jails ever built in this country. It was built in 1881 and is now one of only three remaining. All three are now museums. Rotary jails contained a circular cell structure of considerable size inside of another building that contained only one opening per floor, so that prisoners could only go in or out of their cell once their cell was rotated to the opening, making these jails very secure.

The invention of the rotary jail was intended to improve the safety of the jailers and reduce the contact the inmates had, eliminating plans to break out. There were downsides, which eventually led to the end of these unique jails. Inmates' limbs got caught in the mechanics of the system, and limbs were lost. These jails were also fire hazards. In the event of a fire, there was the danger of not being able to get all the inmates out quickly, considering the cells only allowed one inmate out at a time.

The Rotary Jail Museum is located in Crawfordsville. *W.C. Madden photo.*

The Crawfordsville rotary jail is rumored to have a couple resident ghosts. Pedestrians have passed by when the museum was closed and seen lighted orbs flashing through the windows and even the occasional face peering out. This lured area teens to venture to the property in the late-night hours in an attempt to catch a glimpse of an apparition or to simply have a scare in good fun.

Josh, a Crawfordsville resident, was a teen himself on the night several years ago that he and his friends decided to bring a recorder to call out to the spirits outside the old jail. The group of friends had become fans of the show *Ghost Hunters* on the Syfy channel and started spending their weekends investigating area locations for things that go bump in the night.

The friends had been on several trips before they showed up outside the Rotary Jail Museum and had never really had any paranormal experiences. Thus far, it really had been simply friends having a good time, sharing an adrenaline rush from the possibility of a good scare. On this particular night, no one in the group really believed they would face any real ghostly encounters. None of the teens had ever felt afraid following an investigation, but that was all about to change.

The teens arrived and stood in front of the old courtyard at just past midnight. They chose this location because a hanging had taken place there. Already knowing the rumors of the ghost of the hanged man who haunts the grounds, they were alert, recorder in hand and anxious to see if he would make an appearance.

The teens started calling out to John Coffee's ghost, taunting him to show himself. In 1885, the murdered bodies of James and Mary McMullen were pulled from their home near Elmdale after it had been set on fire to cover up the crime. Authorities arrested twenty-three-year-old John Coffee for the murders. According to his first confession, he went to the McMullens' house. After chatting a while with James, he beat the old man's head, killing him. He then made the old woman tell him where her money was kept, and then he took her outdoors and killed her. He threw her body back into the house and set fire to the building. After nine months with no solution to the murders, citizens were getting uneasy. Since Coffee confessed to the crime three times, it was easy for a jury to convict him of double murder. The judge sentenced him to be executed by hanging.

Coffee became the first person executed in Montgomery County on October 16, 1885. The hanging became a spectacle. Two hundred tickets were sold to onlookers so they could catch a glimpse of the man condemned to death. The onlookers received a horrific fright when the rope broke during the first two tries at hanging Coffee. He was carried up the scaffold, blood flowing from his ears, and finally died on the third try.

Josh and his friends were aware of the rumors suggesting Coffee had an accomplice and was himself innocent of killing the couple. Legend suggests the apparition seen on the grounds is that of Coffee. Coffee implicated James Davis in the murders. Davis was convicted and sentenced to death, but he then appealed and was not convicted. Another rumor is that the spirit in the old courtyard belongs to the sheriff at the time of Coffee's hanging, as he was unable to move on from the possibility of having arrested an innocent man.

Josh and his friends used this information while calling out into the night in an effort to trigger the spirit. They called out for Coffee. They also asked for the sheriff. The night stayed silent—no sudden orbs or anything else appeared.

The teens stayed for about an hour and a half, laughing and having fun attempting to startle each other. Finally, they decided to call it a night and said their goodbyes. John got in his two-door Pontiac Grand Am and headed in the direction of his home, ten minutes away. He turned on the radio and was feeling good after the night of fun, laughing to himself as he reflected on some of the times with his friends. Suddenly, he heard static on the radio; it was on all the stations he turned to. Thinking it was a malfunction, he continued to drive and flipped off the radio. As soon as he did that, the recorder sitting on the seat beside him turned on. This startled Josh. He momentarily lost control of the car. Once he steadied the wheel, he pulled over to the side of the road and picked up the recorder to turn it off. While he was powering it off, a high-pitched noise and static continued for what seemed like an eternity—but was mere seconds—until it finally went quiet. Josh felt the hairs stand up on the back of his neck; his heart raced, and he returned to the road, anxious to get home.

Once home, Josh felt worn out and went to sleep around two in the morning, only to be woken at three-thirty by a loud static and squeaking coming from his clock radio. He distinctly remembers turning it off and making a move to unplug it before stopping himself, deciding if it turned on while unplugged, it would be too much for him. He turned it off and lay awake for a long time, feeling uneasy, before eventually falling back asleep. He awoke again around ten that morning. He sat up and wondered if he had dreamed that the radio had gone off in the middle of the night. It was a new day, and he was determined to move past the creeps he experienced the night before, chalking it up to coincidence and an overactive imagination following a night of paranormal investigating.

As Josh stood up and began to gather his clothes, he froze in place when he noticed his alarm clock, with the cord unplugged, sitting on the dresser—across the room from where it originally was, beside his bed. He could not explain it, but he had a feeling it was related to the night before and the boys taunting the apparitions said to be on the grounds of the Rotary Jail Museum.

A couple hours later, Josh and his two friends from the night before shared the unexplained and eerie situations they all had experienced. One had a horrible nightmare. In the dream, he wasn't able to breathe. He woke up a few times during the night from the same dream. Josh's other friend woke up at three in the morning to his TV turning on, with static and a loud, piercing sound coming from it. When he turned it off, he felt like there was someone else in the room with him, and the temperature suddenly got cold.

After talking through their experiences, not really sure what to believe, they decided to seek the counsel of Josh's uncle, who was a pastor. He advised the boys to return to the jail, apologize and say some prayers.

He gave the teens a firm talking-to about not seeking out the dead but allowing them to rest in peace. Each teen was unnerved and feeling anxious, so trying anything seemed worth the effort.

The next night, Josh and his friends returned to the Rotary Jail Museum at the same time as the previous evening. This time, they offered their apologies and prayed for the souls of those who had suffered and died on the grounds to be at peace. Just like the night before, nothing happened while the teens were on the grounds.

Despite having some anxious nights after this, due to his own fear, Josh reports that he has witnessed no more paranormal activity. In fact, he has not experienced any other first-hand paranormal event since that night at the jail nearly a decade ago. He no longer seeks out the paranormal; he decided he wanted to focus on the living.

One of Josh's friends had a last encounter following their prayer outside the jail. As he drove home that night, he was startled when he passed a man standing on the side of the road with what looked like blood on his face and a rope dangling from his neck. Josh never knew what to make of his friend's story but confesses he is just happy he was not there to see if it was real or an illusion out of fear.

Today, Josh has a deep respect for museums and the history they preserve. He donates to many foundations to preserve and educate others about the past. He believes the paranormal experience he had at the museum helped him grow as a person and increase the respect he has for others. He hopes that sharing his ghostly encounter does not trigger other teenagers to follow his poor judgment but instead motivates others to research and appreciate the events that changed and shaped the community.

The hanging of Coffee, a young man, who may have unjustly been cut short on his life's journey, leaves a lesson for youth to follow: be careful who you hang around and the choices you make. Those who are in a position to impact others' lives by judgments they pass should take the time to give their position the respect it deserves.

Coffee's ghost was reportedly mentioned in newspapers as early as a month after his death. The *Newport Hoosier State*, on October 28, 1885, ran an article reporting that the ghost of Coffee was seen in Elmdale where the murders occurred. The ghost stopped a farmer and rode with him for three miles until he got off and ran at the speed of a jackrabbit before disappearing right across from where the murders took place.

On November 11, 1885, the *Jefferson Daily Evening News* reported that a train conductor saw Coffee's ghost entering the train covered in blood with a noose around his neck. The apparition rode for about thirty miles while others on the train sat paralyzed with fear, before getting off, running up a hill and disappearing.

Stories continue to this day, with alarms going off within the museum when no one is believed to be inside, according to the museum's webpage. In past Octobers, the jail has presented a haunted tour. Ghost stories aside, the museum is a wonderful place to visit and worth the stop the next time you're in Crawfordsville.

UBER GHOST OF CRAWFORDSVILLE

Crawfordsville's history dates back to 1813, when three rangers—Williamson Dunn, Henry Ristine and Major Ambrose Whitlock—thought that the area was an ideal spot for a settlement. Nearly ten years later, the three returned with their families. This community has grown over the years and now has a population numbering about fifteen thousand.

The community is large enough to support a person choosing to make their living as an Uber driver. Seeing the profits that could be made, Marc Miller decided to change jobs, since the years he had spent working in a factory hurt his back and made sleeping at night difficult. He hoped the change would lower his stress levels and keep him off his feet.

Miller had never had an experience with the paranormal and never thought much about it. His new job would change him from a person who gave the paranormal no thought to one who tries not to think about it every time he hears a strange sound.

Driving for Uber introduced him to several people within the community that he may never have talked to before. Miller admitted he began to see that there was a greater issue in the community with drugs and alcoholism than he had assumed. With regret, he reflected that he had to transport several individuals who displayed strange, paranoid and abnormal behavior as a result of meth use.

Having adjusted to the shocking behaviors people exhibited when they were under the influence, Miller didn't think it was unusual when he picked up a large man with a German accent wearing odd clothing and smelling strongly of alcohol outside a historic home on Wabash Avenue. When the man got into the back seat, he didn't say anything to Miller but appeared to be talking in a low voice to himself in German.

Miller asked the man if he still wanted to be taken to the courthouse, confirming the directions he was originally given. Not getting a response, he looked in the rearview mirror and made eye contact with the man, who stared directly at him but said nothing. This caused the hair on Miller's neck to rise, and he had an unexplainable nervous feeling, instinctively knowing something seemed off.

Again, Miller asked the man if the destination was the same, and this time the man gave a muffled-sounding "Yeah." Miller was grateful that it wasn't a long ride and drove his passenger in silence. He recalled with a shaky voice that each time he looked in the rearview mirror, the man was staring at him with hostility in his eyes. This caused Miller to have paranoid thoughts, half expecting the man to pull out a gun any second and demand money from him. After all, the fare had not been paid for, as cash was selected as the payment method for the ride.

After Miller pulled up to the courthouse, the man opened the door and got out without saying a word. Miller hollered at the odd man, as he had not paid. In his frustration, he got out of the car and called out to the man with some foul language as the man continued to walk away. The man stopped suddenly and glared at Miller with icy cold eyes. Miller immediately froze as the man disappeared inside the building. He was feeling angry and upset with himself for even allowing the cash option when, suddenly, he got a notification that his Uber customer, the one he had just dropped off, was wanting to know Miller's expected time of arrival.

Miller was shocked to learn the man he picked up was not the customer who requested his services. He called the actual customer, who was still waiting his arrival, and explained what had happened and caused his delay, but he received no information on the call regarding who he had picked up. Miller was still feeling a little unnerved when he got home later that evening, but he tried to forget it as he sat down to eat takeout and watch a movie with his girlfriend.

As the night moved on, Miller laughed at the comedy flick they were watching, and he had completely forgotten about the strange man who stiffed him by the time he went to bed. He woke up at about two-thirty in the morning to his girlfriend shaking him. She was clearly upset and shaking as he got up and turned on the light. His girlfriend told him that she woke up, feeling extremely cold and uneasy. When she opened her eyes, a large man was standing there glaring down at her. He didn't say anything or seem to be aware of her. A second later, he was gone.

Miller had not told his girlfriend anything about the man who stiffed him other than to vent briefly after he got home that someone had not paid him. Miller said that his girlfriend described the man as wearing the same clothing Miller had seen him in, a button-up gray shirt and suspenders. Miller told her the man also had on very distinctive black pants made of a heavy, odd material, but his girlfriend hadn't been able to make out the man's pants in the dark. What stood out to Miller the most was that as she settled down after telling him what she'd seen, they both suddenly began to smell alcohol.

It took weeks for the couple to not feel uneasy as they slept at night, and Miller half expected they would have an encounter with the man again. To his relief, almost two years later, he has not had any more glimpses of or encounters with the angry German spirit.

Miller no longer lives in Crawfordsville, yet he has developed an interest in the area's history. While learning about the area's early days, Miller discovered there was a German business owner who ran a brewery and saloon not far from the courthouse in the 1800s. He has often wondered if this could have some connection to the encounter he had. Miller has never found the courage to look further into it for fear of getting the unwanted attention of a violent male spirit. He got on the bad side of this apparition enough for it to follow him. He now totally believes in spirits.

CHAPTER 12
MIAMI COUNTY

TILLET CEMETERY KNOWN BY ANOTHER NAME

In the city of Peru sits Tillet Cemetery, but it goes by another name that's ghostly—Hookman's Cemetery.

A ghostly story accompanies the name. Supposedly, a man with a hook for a hand wanders the nearby roads in search of his victims. Sometimes there are thick, eerie fogs and cold spots that are creepy.

One person went to the cemetery one night. It got foggy and cold, and they saw the man with the hook as well as a cat's head in a tree and its body sitting on top of a rock.

One person has gone there many times and has had many different experiences. He feels like he is being watched by someone. One July evening, he went to the cemetery with another person. As they entered the cemetery, they felt cold and could see their breaths; however, it was July and not cold at all. The ghost hunter instantly got goosebumps. The two heard footsteps and sticks breaking, but they saw nobody. The hunter started to tell the other person that there were quite a few Tillets buried in the cemetery, hence the name. When he said "few," he heard a voice speak out, but the other person heard nothing.

The two decided to leave, and after they got some distance from the cemetery, the air was much warmer. As they walked down the trail, they felt like they were being followed.

Another person who lived in the woods near the cemetery saw a ghostly face in their bedroom window one night. They heard horses running down the hill. The next morning, they found their hound dogs dead in the cemetery, but there was no blood or wounds on the animals.

PEACEFUL ACRES NOT SO PEACEFUL

Peaceful Acres Mobile Home Park in Peru isn't so peaceful at night, according to the Will County Ghost Hunters Society.

The ghost of a man wearing a bandanna has been seen in the woods and floating over a chicken coop. The man has been nicknamed "the toothless wonder."

The park contains less than a dozen mobile homes and is located off U.S. 31 south of Peru at 5485 U.S. 31 South.

The sign for Peaceful Acres is somewhat ghostly, as it has all but faded away over the years. *W.C. Madden photo.*

SLAUGHTER HOUSE ROAD

Slaughter House Road in Macy is haunted by the old abandoned slaughterhouse, according to the Will County Ghost Hunters Society.

People have reported seeing apparitions of cows in and near the buildings. They have heard sounds of cows crying out as if they were being slaughtered. Farmers have reported that their livestock have been killed right in their own pastures.

The slaughterhouse was located down a narrow gravel road on the east side of U.S. 31 about two miles southwest of Macy; however, it doesn't seem to be there anymore.

MYSTERIOUS HOUSE

The Old Stone House in Peru is haunted, according to the Will County Ghost Hunters Society.

The house was part of the Underground Railroad during the Civil War when slaves were escaping from the South. It caught fire several years ago and was abandoned. People have reported strange and mysterious lights coming from inside the house.

HAUNTED HOUSE AND BARN

A house and barn that once stood in Plevna was haunted, according to the Will County Ghost Hunters Society.

People have seen the apparition of a woman in white and bright red orbs moving around the grounds. The house used to be called the Ferrell House.

CHAPTER 13
NEWTON COUNTY

STRANGE VISITORS TO FOSTER PARK IN GOODLAND

When a parent takes their children to play at the park, it is not unusual for their kids to make instant friends with other children and play happily. But the parent probably doesn't expect to meet someone they feel they have known all their lives. While on a visit to Foster Park in Goodland with her two children one sunny afternoon, something strange happened to Melinda, a thirty-something stay-at-home mom.

Melinda lives in Kentland and often visits the park while her husband fishes nearby on the weekends. Normally, she will play a game on her phone or bring a book to read while her children enjoy the park. On this particular day, she said the sky was a vivid blue and the temperature was particularly warm. She was surprised when she noticed a middle-aged woman walking toward her in what appeared to be a Victorian-era costume, perhaps for a reenactment, that was far too hot for the day's weather.

As the woman got closer, Melinda began to smell the scent of lavender. The woman lowered her head, nodded and raised her eyes in a gesture of saying hello as she approached. Curiosity getting the best of her, Melinda responded, asking her if there was some kind of historical event happening today. Immediately, she felt rude for having been so direct without so much as saying hello to the woman, but she was relieved when the woman's response was pleasant. The woman let out a soft laugh and said no, not

Foster Park is located in Goodland. *Dorothy Salvo Benson photo.*

to her knowledge. She then introduced herself as Idella Turner. Melinda exchanged introductions and apologized for her question. She also explained how surprised she was to see Idella dressed as she was. Smoothing out her long skirt, Idella responded that she was wearing her most comfortable attire for a stroll.

Although Melinda thought that a little odd, there was something very pleasant and calming about the woman, and they continued to talk. The time passed quickly, and the two women chatted like old friends about gardening, recipes and raising kids. Melinda learned that Idella was from Illinois originally and had several children. In reflection, Melinda stated she found nothing unusual about the conversation, aside from one odd comment.

When the ladies were talking about their children, Idella said that she felt very fortunate that all her children made it to adulthood. Thinking Idella must have started her family very young for her kids to all be adults, she asked her if her children all lived nearby. Idella responded, "They did all go off, and we were apart for some time, but we are all together again." She smiled and seemed to have an inner contentment that Melinda admired; Melinda did not press her for more answers.

Melinda shared that she was looking forward to next summer and a big family trip they were planning to the Canadian side of Niagara Falls. Melinda explained they had planned on going last summer, but the coronavirus caused them to put their plans on hold, as Canada was closed to vacationers. Idella listened, smiled and nodded, simply telling Melinda her own family came from Canada originally, and she had heard talk about the falls and the fascination people had with them.

When Melinda looked at her phone, she noticed they had been talking for over an hour, and she hollered at her children to come over and get something to drink. As the children ran toward them, Melinda unzipped the small cooler she had brought and asked Idella if she would like some water. Getting no response, she looked up, and all she saw was her two children, who had just approached. Idella was gone.

Melinda asked her children if they saw where the woman that she was just talking to went. She was baffled, as Idella seemed to have disappeared in a flicker of a second. The children replied that they hadn't seen anybody. Melinda went on to describe the woman to the children. Their response only further alarmed her, confirming that their visit to the park today was anything but normal.

The children, whom Melinda had been watching play as she engaged in her conversation, told their mother they saw no adult wearing an old-fashioned long dress anywhere at the park today; however, their two new friends, who were about the same age as them, also wore long dresses and hats. Melinda had not seen them playing with anyone, so she asked the children where their friends were right now. The children were not alarmed but simply said they didn't see them now, and they must have gone home.

Melinda asked the kids what their new friends' names were, but they couldn't recall exactly. They only said that their friends were nice and smelled like flowers. Melinda recalled the lavender scent she first smelled when Idella approached her. She admitted that prior to this particular day, she had never seen a ghost or really given any thought to whether ghosts were something she believed in or not.

Following the day at the park, Melinda said she tried to look up her new friend on the computer. She hoped to find an address and phone number. She wanted to ask Idella why she ran off without saying a quick goodbye.

Melinda rationalized to herself that the children's account of their new friends could have been triggered by her asking them about seeing Idella and her description of the woman. After all, kids have a different perception of things and vivid imaginations. She knew she was not making sense, but there had to be a reasonable explanation. After all, she knew she was not talking to herself for over an hour, and she recalled Idella in detail. She even remembered her unique name.

All rational explanations were lost to Melinda, until she discovered there was an Idella who had lived in Goodland but had passed away on September 11, 1945. The Idella she found had the last name Hall. She had nine children and was once married to a Turner. Another thing that stood out to Melinda was that Idella Hall, who was born on April 7, 1866, was from Illinois and had Canadian parents. It seemed impossible, but this Idella did apparently have a lot in common with the lady Melinda talked to in the park.

There seemed to be more questions than answers for Melinda as she reflected on her meeting with Idella. Also, she could not make sense of how the two young girls in period clothing that her children claimed they played with were connected to her own encounter. Idella had said her own children made it to adulthood. Could there have been other visitors from the past enjoying the park that day? One question Melinda can now answer is: Does she believe in life after death? The short and direct response she gives is, "Absolutely."

ANOTHER LIFE, ANOTHER TIME

Sometimes people experience a paranormal occurrence that has nothing to do with an apparition or an entity. The Oxford Dictionary defines *paranormal* as "supernatural or inexplicable by the laws of science or reason—an experience that defies explanation." That is exactly what happened to Margarita Ramirez when she first came to Kentland.

Ramirez grew up in Mexico, and from the time she was a young girl, she has had an obsession with the American Midwest. When she was three years old, she told her mother and grandmother that she remembered her other family who lived in America. She would have dreams of a large house and the belongings inside it. She vividly recalled images of people from an era she would come to identify as an adult as the 1920s and 1930s.

Ramirez would wake up from her dreams calling out for a mother different from the one she knew. This confused her as a child, and she soon came to believe it was nothing more than her imagination, as she was told. Over the years, the images faded, but the strange fascination with the Midwest stayed with her. When she had the opportunity as a teenager to move to America, she was thrilled. She learned they were moving to Indiana to be with family.

A strange energy stirred inside her, and she knew it was for a reason bigger than simply the excitement that comes with change. She felt like she was going home. Ramirez is a very religious person and never associated her obsession or pull toward America with anything paranormal. She believed it was just the direction God was sending her in.

The day Ramirez first arrived within miles of Kentland, an odd feeling overcame her. She felt like she had been there before. The sensation of déjà vu triggered her, and all her senses came alert. She sat quietly in the back seat, looking out the window as her pulse raced faster than ever. Ramirez can distinctly recall breaking out in a cold sweat, even though the day was comfortable and there was no air conditioning on in the vehicle.

When they passed the courthouse, Ramirez felt overwhelmed and then became dizzy. She started crying out for her uncle to stop the car. When he pulled over, she got out immediately and was shaking. The feeling of déjà vu turned into more than a feeling that she had been there before. She absolutely knew she had been there before. A flood of images came to her. She began to talk too fast and gasped for air while telling her family what she was experiencing.

Ramirez could vividly remember another life in which she was walking across the courthouse lawn arm in arm with a man in a uniform. In the memory, she looked different, but she knew it was herself; the man was unknown to her. She knew they had a feeling of sadness between them at that moment.

Ramirez's family soothed her, but to her surprise, they listened and gave her support. Her uncle suggested that maybe she was remembering another life, and that was when the idea of reincarnation first came to her as a possibility. Over the last few years, she has made her home in Jasper County, not far from Kentland in Newton County. She moved slightly away from Kentland because the emotional pull of memories in shadows just beyond her reach was too much for her. Feeling a need to focus on her life today and live healthily, she no longer looked back, trying to solve the mysteries of her past. However, at night, she dreams about the man in the uniform. She awakens having to shake off the feeling of loss.

Margarita Ramerez has lived a full life, working hard cleaning homes to care for her family, and she has no regrets about moving to Indiana. Her husband returned to Mexico a few years back, and she has chosen to stay. She feels strongly that if there is such a thing as soulmates who travel together throughout lifetimes, here is where she will find hers once again.

CHAPTER 14
PULASKI COUNTY

THE MYSTERIOUS MOODY LIGHTS

For a long time, there have been legends about some mysterious lights that appear on old Moody Road, which is west of Francesville toward Rensselaer. You won't find the road on Google Maps because the name has changed to Meridian Road. You have to go at night and park at the *T* of Meridian and Division Roads, which is south of where Indiana 49 ends. Then flash your lights three times. You should see a light scanning the field.

Several legends have developed over the years about what causes the strange lights. One legend has it that old man Moody's youngest daughter took the horse and buggy to Francesville one night and never returned. He went out to look for her and found that she had lost control of the buggy and crashed into a tree. The light seen by many is supposed to be Mr. Moody with his lantern, looking for his lost daughter. Another legend has it that it was his son and not his daughter.

Another tale told by Abulia Productions in a video in 2013 has it that two brothers were returning from northwest Indiana when a thunderstorm arrived, scaring the horses. The older brother went for help while the younger brother stayed with the horses. When the brother returned, he discovered his brother had been killed and his head was decapitated and lying in a cornfield. The light is a lantern he is using to search for his brother's murderer.

This is the intersection of Division and Meridian Roads. Meridian Road used to be called Moody Road; people have seen strange lights there at night. *W.C. Madden photo.*

Another legend has it that old man Moody was traveling down the road in his buggy when he fell off the buggy and it decapitated him. The light is someone looking for his head. If you believe this story, I have some land in Florida you might be interested in buying.

People have explained the lights as car lights coming from Indiana 49 to the north. Some have even said it's swamp gas, according to ObscUrban Legend Wikia. Bill Moncell, who lived in that area as a child, went to see the lights several times and never witnessed them. He said a group from Purdue University came out to investigate the strange lights and had no idea where they could be coming from.

There's also Smith Graveyard nearby on Country Road 300 West near West 100 South. A man and a woman were supposedly killed on opposite sides of the road near it. Supposedly, at midnight, you can see the woman crossing the road to see her man, according to Indiana Ghost Hunters.

CHAPTER 15
TIPPECANOE COUNTY

HISTORIC GREENBUSH CEMETERY HAUNTED

Greenbush Cemetery is Lafayette's oldest cemetery. To the traffic from the nearby street, it appears to be a historic and tranquil resting place. Peaceful and well cared for, the Greenbush Cemetery is a nice place for a quiet stroll or, for history lovers, a great place to explore. On a warm, sunny day, the cemetery invites you to walk under the shade trees and read the headstones of some of the area's notable historical citizens.

Danielle, a thirty-something Lafayette-area resident, was walking her dog just past the cemetery on a bright and warm summer day around three in the afternoon when she stopped dead in her tracks. Looking into the cemetery, she saw a man in early twentieth-century clothing walking with his head down at a determined pace. What startled her is that he seemed to walk right through the headstones.

Danielle blinked several times, trying to clear her vision, believing herself to be seeing things. At this point, her dog began to bark and tried to pull her in the direction of the man. The dog's barking captured the attention of the man, who stopped suddenly and vanished. Before Danielle could even gasp, the man reappeared directly in front of her on the sidewalk. He was not much taller than her five feet, six inches. She was frozen where she stood, and even her dog became eerily still. The man was thin and wore a long brown coat with a belt around it, despite the warm weather.

The man's eyes met Danielle's, and they were a striking blue. She picked up a seriousness about him. He raised his hand, pulled down on the front of his newsboy-style cap and nodded, in a gesture that said he was apologetic for startling her. Danielle braced herself, expecting him to suddenly disappear once again, but to her surprise, he casually strolled past her, whistling as he went.

Fear overcame her. She could not force herself to look back in his direction, and she walked quickly away from the cemetery. It has been several years since she experienced her ghostly encounter, and she confesses that she has never worked up the nerve to walk past the park again.

Danielle is only one of many who have had ghostly encounters at the historic cemetery. The cemetery is filled with notable headstones, including those of judges, entrepreneurs and other important people in Lafayette history. It is also the final resting place of twenty-two Union soldiers who were on their way home from the war when their train crashed on Halloween night in 1864. There have been several reports of people seeing a soldier in a Union uniform walking along the fence line near the graves of these soldiers who never made it home. There are also thirty-eight Confederate soldiers buried in the cemetery. They were captured and brought to a prison camp in Lafayette.

Crystal, a nurse in Lafayette, was heading home after a long shift when she passed the cemetery in the early morning hours. She had lowered the window of her sports utility vehicle, allowing the cool morning air in to help revive her in her exhausted state. First, she smelled burning oil. Then she saw three men in what appeared to be Civil War–era uniforms.

At first, she thought she was seeing some kind of reenactment. She noticed that the men appeared to be standing at attention and looking at something. She said it was only a brief moment, but it is embedded in her memory because of what happened next. A sudden flash of very bright light occurred, and the men were gone. Crystal admits that she was very tired but notes she was fully functional, as most nurses function on little sleep. She is fully confident she witnessed a paranormal occurrence in the cemetery.

Not all paranormal ghostly encounters are recognized when they happen. There are times when it takes years for one to realize they experienced something not of this world. On a comfortable fall day, nearly seventeen years ago, a brother and sister encountered a kind act from a peculiar pedestrian in the cemetery that, years later, changed their views on life after death.

Chris was thirteen and his sister eleven the day they entered the cemetery in the late afternoon. Chris shared that he and his sister were taking a walk

This monument at Greenbush Cemetery honors the thirty-eight Confederate soldiers who perished in a train accident. *W.C. Madden photo.*

through the cemetery, reading the old headstones and poking fun at each other. They were having a good time and enjoying the outdoor adventure.

At one point, they began to run, in an attempt to see who could reach the fence first. Chris's sister tripped and fell hard on the ground. She began to cry as she sat up and, immediately, blood started gushing from her nose. Feeling concerned for his sister, Chris tried to see if she was injured and to calm her down.

Suddenly, two black, highly polished men's shoes appeared in front of them. "Can I assist?" a well-spoken male voice asked the two startled siblings. Chris stood up, noting that the man in front of them was finely dressed, wearing a suit with a high-neck collar in a style he had never seen before. Chris explained to the man that his sister had fallen and her nose wouldn't stop bleeding.

The man kneeled down and introduced himself as Dr. Wetherill. He had a natural way of making both siblings feel at ease. He gently took out a handkerchief from inside his jacket and handed it to Chris's sister. Then he instructed her to hold her head back and pinch the cloth against her nose. The doctor instructed Chris to take her home and prescribed rest, assuring them she would be just fine.

Chris and his sister thanked the stranger for his help and headed for home. At the time, they didn't think there was anything paranormal about their encounter with the man. It was years later, when Chris was a student at Purdue University, that he would receive a chill down his spine when he was reminded of that fall day in Greenbush Cemetery. The R.B. Wetherill Laboratory of Chemistry at Purdue University is the connecting thread that introduced Chris to the belief that life does not end with death.

While doing some research on the campus's history for a class assignment, Chris was jolted when he came across the picture of a Dr. Richard Benbridge Wetherill, after whom the chemistry building is named. He felt his heart begin to race and sweat break out on the back of his neck as he stared at the familiar face of Dr. Wetherill in the old black-and-white photo. He was brought back to the day at the cemetery when a man introduced himself as Dr. Wetherill. One particular image of the man's starched white collar, high around his neck, stood out to Chris. The man in the photo looked exactly like the doctor who had helped them, and he wore the same style of dress.

Chris showed the picture to his sister, and she was extremely uncomfortable, expressing that she did not want to talk about it. Chris also learned that Dr. Wetherill's final resting place is in Greenbush Cemetery. He has no idea if they had been near the doctor's grave when they were at the cemetery and does not even recall seeing a headstone with the doctor's name on it.

According to the Tippecanoe County Historical Association website, Dr. Wetherill was a very respected and accomplished doctor and businessman. He was the founder and first president of the historical association and had a passion for travel and history, taking part in several archaeological digs and studying ancient peoples. The doctor was one of the few people who were the first outsiders to view the remains found in the final resting place of the boy king, King Tutankhamun. This was a huge honor and further hinted at the remarkable man the doctor was.

Chris has never gathered the courage to return to the Greenbush Cemetery and see if he can run into the good doctor once again. Instead, he feels he can attest from his personal experience to what a kind and caring man the doctor was when he chose to appear to the siblings and offer help. Chris is convinced the doctor continues to watch over the community he considers home, despite all his world travels.

Dr. Wetherill's is not the only ghost story connected to the chemistry building at Purdue. Many have reported receiving assistance from a thin man in a white shirt sporting a pocket protector full of pens. It is, in fact, the pocket protector, no longer commonly seen, that identifies the helpful man as being the same person in several different reports.

Sarah was new to Purdue in the fall of 2011, and the large campus was very intimidating to her. She was experiencing high anxiety most days, fearful of being late for her classes in her attempts to recall how to get to each one. She was from a small town and had never lived in such a highly populated area, making her even more anxious when she left her dorm.

Sarah confesses that on her second day of classes, she allowed her anxiety to overwhelm her. She was running late for her chemistry class and got completely turned around, confused about which direction she was to go. She sat down on the ground outside the chemistry building and began to have a panic attack. She began to think irrationally. She had thoughts of calling her mom and asking her to take her back home.

Suddenly, Sarah smelled aftershave and looked up to see a slender man, wearing high-waisted pants with a belt and a crisp white shirt and bow tie, smiling at her. "You look like you could use some help," he said.

Sarah can't explain it, but she recalls feeling suddenly calm and relaxed. She described the man as being in his late fifties and having kind eyes. He wore a pocket protector, which stood out to her as something you don't see every day. He had an easygoing nature and made some jokes about first-year jitters. He helped Sarah recognize she was not alone in feeling overwhelmed; it was a normal part of adjusting to a new environment. She recalls the man as being very rational in understanding what she was going through, without her even telling him.

The man pointed Sarah in the direction of her class. She felt renewed as she turned to walk in the direction he was pointing. Then she realized she hadn't thanked him, so she stopped and turned around, but he was gone. At the time, she gave it no thought and hurried to her class. She began to settle into the daily routine of getting to her classes, and her anxiety dissipated following her encounter with the man.

Sarah continued her studies, and it was not until her third year that she heard a girl in one of her classes share a paranormal encounter that she had in the chemistry building. Sarah's classmate told those who were listening about a friendly older man in a white shirt who had helped direct her. She described him as wearing a pocket protector and glasses. Sarah's interest immediately came to attention at the mention of the pocket protector; it reminded her of the man who had helped calm her. She confessed that she did not recall him wearing glasses, but the rest of the description sounded the same.

When Sarah's classmate mentioned that the man turned and walked into a wall, disappearing right after talking to her, Sarah was suddenly triggered to remember how fast the man disappeared after helping her. It really brought home the belief she had herself. Sarah realized she had experienced a paranormal encounter when her classmate pulled out a picture of former professor M. Guy Mellon. She recognized him as the same man who helped her regain control and lower her anxiety.

Mellon was hired at Purdue in 1919 to teach analytical chemistry and remained active in the department for years. Professor Mellon and his wife, Catherine, were said to be very socially active in welcoming new students to adjust to campus life. According to the Purdue University Chemistry website, after Mellon's death in 1993 (just shy of his 100th birthday), the Professor M. Guy Mellon Scholarship was established in 2008, and the Amy-Mellon Lectureship in Analytical Chemistry was established in 1988.

HAUNTED SCHOOL

A ghostly figure of a man passing from window to window has been reported at Cumberland Elementary School in West Lafayette, according to the Will County Ghost Hunters Society. The reason it couldn't be a living person is that it goes from window to window in seconds, and this would require it to walk through walls. The Cumberland School is now called the West Lafayette Elementary School.

Cumberland Elementary School, now West Lafayette Elementary School, has had a ghostly figure passing from window to window. *W.C. Madden photo.*

HAUNTED HARRISON CEMETERY

Visitors to Harrison Cemetery, also known as Pierce Cemetery, in West Lafayette have reported hearing crying and moaning along with eerie feelings that someone is watching them, according to Indiana Haunted Houses (indianahauntedhouses.com).

A few people have said they were even touched by something unseen or have had things thrown at them by invisible hands. The gravestones are said to move around as well.

A group of seven went to the cemetery to check it out and said they did many EVP sessions and got a lot of responses, according to the Haunted Hovel (hauntedhovel.com). They heard a voice that said, "Caroline." They found a broken headstone that read "Caroline." They heard a man say "Rebecca" and found a Rebecca's gravestone located there. They also got a spike on their K2 meter in a corner of the cemetery.

The local television station in Lafayette, WLFI-TV, did a report on the cemetery in 2019. Justin Arnett, founder of the nonprofit 765 Paranormal, said they caught EVPs of gunshots and old musket shots. Several Civil War

Harrison Cemetery, a very old cemetery with graves dating back to the 1840s, has sustained a lot of damage, and many gravestones have fallen over. *W.C. Madden photo.*

veterans are buried there. They caught an EVP of someone saying, "I'm from Hell."

The small cemetery is located behind the William Henry Harrison High School at 5701 North 50 West in rural West Lafayette. It is very dark at night, since it's located behind the school.

RESIDUAL HAUNTING AT PURDUE

It was nearing nine-thirty at night, and the college student sat alone in his dorm room. The room was dimly lit, and he sat leaning forward over his Spanish text, trying to commit to memory the words on the pages. Honestly, he was struggling to keep his eyes open.

The student had not been sleeping well since moving into the dorm and woke several times during the nights. He can't say why he woke, but he had come to realize over the first few weeks that his wake time was always at one-thirty and four-thirty in the morning. Not 1:29 a.m., but exactly half past the hour.

His roommate seemed to be unaffected by the transition to dorm living, and he always slept through the night. What unnerved the student, who wants to remain anonymous, was the sensation he got when he woke up. This eerie feeling that he was not alone made him freeze where he lay. He sensed a heightened energy in the room that made him feel anxious, causing his heart to race. He often forced his eyes to stay shut and just listened to the sound of the fan in the room as he attempted to drift back to sleep. It usually took about fifteen minutes to half an hour for this rush of energy to dissipate.

On other occasions, the student would feel his dorm room suddenly shake, as if there was an explosion nearby. This particular occurrence was experienced by his roommate as well. It happened several times, and the lights flickered, too.

This particular night, as he sat studying for a Spanish test, he became suddenly alert when a cold breeze blew across the back of his neck. He froze where he sat and gave himself an internal pep talk that it was nothing. He was being paranoid. The sensation that he was not alone in his dorm room overcame the inner voice that was persuading him to relax. He took some deep breaths, trying to steady his increasing heartbeat, and he kept his eyes downcast on the book below. Thoughts swarmed his mind, and he tried to

Wiley Hall may have a residual haunting due to a murder. *Dorothy Salvo Benson photo.*

reassure himself that there were many other people inside the dorm beyond the walls of his room. He really was not alone, and there were many within earshot if he were to scream. Then he began to reason with himself. How embarrassed would he be if he ran from his room in fear? He began to calm down. He was not a small boy afraid of the dark. He was an adult sitting in his dorm room with nothing at all to be afraid of.

"Turn the page," said the voice, which was male and demanding, in a low tone. It was coming from right behind him. The student jumped up with eyes closed, afraid to look. He felt his way toward the door. He no longer cared if he made a spectacle of himself. There was, without question, an unseen being directly behind him in his room. When he made it to the hallway, he felt something rush past him before hearing a door slam a moment later. Immediately following, he felt that rumble, and the floor of the corridor and the wall he was leaning against vibrated with the force of a nearby explosion.

That was the experience of a former resident of Wiley Hall on the Purdue University campus in West Lafayette. He resided in an all-male dorm his first year before moving off campus to live in an apartment. The young man struggled during his first year to adjust to the odd occurrences. Having nowhere else to go, he forced himself to accept what he could not understand and control his fear.

At the end of his first semester, while eating in the dining court, he overheard another student sharing similar experiences to those he was having. He joined the conversation and was stunned to learn that the group believed they had an explanation for the occurrences.

According to news reports, in October 1996, Jarrod Allen Eskew, eighteen, of Crawfordsville, walked into Wiley Hall, a men's dormitory housing mainly freshmen. He entered the third-floor room of Jay Severson, a twenty-seven-year-old graduate student from Fair Oaks, and shot him twice. After killing him, he immediately returned to his room, closed the door and killed himself.

Severson had turned in Eskew for cocaine use, and this was believed to be what motivated the crime. Cocaine use gives a person a rush of energy that can last up to thirty minutes; this mimics the feeling the freshman was having when he woke at night. The sound of the gunshot may have left an imprint of its vibration within the rooms of Wiley Hall, creating a residual haunting that repeats throughout time.

GHOSTS IN BATTLE GROUND

The town of Battle Ground is the site of some important Native American history, including the famous Battle of Tippecanoe and the Trail of Death, which passes nearby. It is not surprising that the location has become a hot spot of paranormal phenomena. Many have claimed to see Native American warriors as well as soldiers in the area of the battlefield. Others have experienced apparitions and shadows in various locations throughout the Battle Ground community.

Joshua DeWitt had heard stories of ghostly apparitions being seen on the battlefield and nearby at Prophet's Rock, but he never gave them much thought. He confesses he never had an interest in ghost stories and local lore.

DeWitt is an outdoorsman who enjoys fishing and riding his motorcycle. If someone mentions racing or baseball, he is all ears, but when it came to the subject of science fiction or paranormal encounters, he would lose interest. The key word is *would*, as he no longer feels that way. Now, if someone mentions a ghostly encounter, DeWitt is all ears, clinging to his own need to feel validated by others having had a similar experience. This need followed DeWitt's own paranormal encounter on a fall afternoon in November 2020, as he walked along the Wabash River not far from the location of the Battle of Tippecanoe.

Like many people in the fall of 2020, DeWitt was feeling cooped up after the several months he had already spent working from home as a result of the COVID-19 pandemic sweeping the globe. To help reduce the growing depression he felt from so much time spent home alone, DeWitt would take a day or two every week to go out and explore nature by driving to nearby parks and walking.

The air was cool but felt good, making him fully alert and revived as he walked along the water's edge. He was thinking about things he had to do during in the week ahead and enjoying himself when he heard someone breathing hard and running in his direction. He saw a man with long dark hair, appearing to be Native American, carrying what looked like an old kind of rifle. The man was dressed in a loincloth, leggings and an old-fashioned men's dress shirt and vest.

DeWitt was baffled and felt uncomfortable as the man came closer. He shared that in the less than fifteen seconds it took the man to approach him, there were several thoughts that passed through his mind. He wondered why the man was running. He also remembered that the parking lot was empty when he pulled in, and there were no gatherings because of COVID, so a historical event was out of the question.

As the man came within a foot of DeWitt, his face paint stood out, giving the impression of someone who should not be messed with. Then the intimidating figure made eye contact with DeWitt. It was obvious that he saw DeWitt, as he moved around him. Then he actually ran into the water, despite the cold temperatures.

DeWitt screamed for the man to stop. He's not sure why he did it. This seemed to capture the man's full attention. He looked at DeWitt, nodded and threw his rifle in DeWitt's direction. Out of instinct, DeWitt reached up with both hands to grab it, but he was stunned when it dissolved right as he was about to close his hands around the weapon. It had simply vanished into thin air.

DeWitt brought his attention back to the man standing in the water a few feet away. The man also began to dissolve. Dewitt felt his heart race and actually had to steady himself as his knees began to shake. Looking around, he saw no one else nearby.

The trip back to his car was one of short steps followed by sprints, then stopping to make sure no one was watching him. DeWitt has absolutely no explanation for what he experienced, but he does know it was real and did happen to him.

BATTLEGROUNDS HAUNTED

The Battle Field Memorial at Battle Ground is supposedly haunted. People have reported seeing men running through the memorial and the creek.

This plaque honors Major Joseph Hamilton Daviess, who died in the Battle of Tippecanoe. *W.C. Madden photo.*

There have been numerous reports of people screaming and feeling cold spots on warm days.

The Battle of Tippecanoe was fought there on November 11, 1811. American forces lost thirty-seven men in the battle, and the Native Americans lost many men but fewer than the Americans. Some days later, the Native Americans returned to the battlefield to find their dead had been scalped and mutilated, so they dug up the solders and did the same to them.

A GHOSTLY ENCOUNTER INSPIRES

Life is about more than our day-to-day persona, such as the image we portray and the job we hold. Life is about getting to know our true self, as we are today, and discovering how we can grow into a better person tomorrow. None of us know where life will take us or when our time will come, but when we choose to challenge ourselves, it will have a large impact on the road we travel. One's mindset regarding life can determine the quality of life one experiences.

Even with the best of intentions, when we take on more than we can handle, the result is not our very best. "I've come to consider all the different views, thoughts, and questions regarding what I prioritize in my life," shared Sarah of Lafayette. "Just as daily living problems require focus and patience, so does finding happiness. Finding the right formulas for your life leads to the reward of that aha moment when you realize: 'By George, I got it.'"

Sarah is a single mother of three and found that when she took on too much, there was a disconnection in her life. Running in multiple directions resulted in less than her very best performance. She said,

What I'm about to tell you will sound crazy, but it is true, and it changed my life. I'm learning that there will always be things that need to be achieved and responsibilities that need to be attended to. Staying present in the now is my new life motto. Here is where it gets a bit nuts. I got this inspirational change of thinking...from a ghost.

Sarah was living in the Bluffs Apartments in Lafayette when she had her paranormal experience there. She describes it not with fear in her voice but as an inspirational intervention. It all began one morning when she could not find her keys. She explained,

I was running late as usual and getting more frustrated by the minute running around the house looking for my keys. I always set them on a shelf by the door. This morning, they were not there, and I was snapping at the children, thinking one of them had moved them. Finally, I found them in a bin full of outdoor sports gear in the closet. Not thinking anymore about it, I rushed to start my day. This was just the first of many days with things disappearing and me blaming the kids.

Over the next several months, things would disappear from where she last saw them, only to reappear somewhere unusual. Her keys would be found in a pair of her hiking boots, her phone was misplaced in a summer beach basket way up high where the kids could not reach, or her purse was found in an empty old picnic basket she used for decorations. It just made no sense to her, and she was convinced one of her kids was doing it on purpose.

"The scavenger hunt became an infuriating daily routine, and I began to wonder if one of my kids needed help, if they were acting out for attention," explained Sarah. "I was very busy, and my separation from their father was never really talked about. He just kinda left, and life went on, busier than ever."

One afternoon, when Sarah was at work, she got a call from her son's school that he was very sick and had a suddenly spiked fever and stomach pains. When she picked him up, the school nurse suggested she get him to the doctor as soon as possible, as she worried it could be something needing immediate treatment. The nurse's suspicions were correct; his appendix needed to be taken out right away. "As I sat there waiting, in a state of shock and worry, my mind raced. I could not remember the last things I said to him that morning before school or if he had any symptoms I should have noticed," Sarah said, looking down with a mother's embarrassment.

Sarah had been so busy and worried about tomorrow, she realized she could not recall the last time she just played with her kids. She sat with tears filling her eyes in that cold hospital waiting area, consumed by guilt. How had her life gotten to this point—where she could not even remember the last thing she said to her kids that morning? Sarah said,

> *I really was about to lose it when suddenly an older man, who smelled like Brut cologne, was sitting in a chair across from me. I remember the atmosphere had changed. I mean, I can't really put it in words, but I felt calmed. He smiled at me and just began to talk to me. He never even commented or asked why I had been crying or why I was there. He just shared a funny story about when his son was young. I really can't remember how he started it, but I really focused on when he shared that his son passed away years earlier at only nine years old. I told him how sad and hard that must have been, but he smiled and said he had so many moments that were good and so many memories that he could not be angry or feel resentment. He talked some more, and I began to find myself thinking of all the things I wanted to do with my kids as he shared his family memories of his son.*

Sarah smiled and sat quietly for a few minutes, lost in thought, before continuing,

> *Here is where my ghost story begins, I guess you can say. I asked him where he stayed when he went to the Dunes [when] he had such a great time, expressing I would like to take my children. He sat back in his chair and smiled, telling me he was so happy he could inspire me and it was nice to hear a young mother planning to slow down and enjoy time with her children. Then he said the oddest thing. He told me to be sure and pack my hiking shoes for some of the trails and bring lots of outdoor games for the kids, because it was a great place to play ball with the kids in the Chesterton Indiana Dunes beaches. Then he winked at me, saying that I had better take a backpack to carry my phone and keys, because it would be awful to lose them on the trails. I thought that was unusual and was about to say something, but I heard the hospital corridor electric door open and turned to look in the direction. A split second later, turning my head back to the friendly old man across from me, I was taken aback to find he had completely disappeared!*

There could be a rational explanation for why he disappeared. Sarah was in an emotional state, and he could have quickly stood and moved around the corner without her noticing. It was his words that haunted her. Her lost keys, phone and purse over the months leading up to that moment had all been recovered in the items he suggested she bring with her. Sarah has no exciting end to her ghost story, no reappearing of the old man or spooky connection; however, she later discovered an old man had died in her apartment. Her items have never disappeared again.

A belief in prioritizing what matters most is a personal journey that Sarah has developed and lived by since her encounter. Her son fully recovered, and the family went on to have family fun nights and mealtime as part of their weekly routine. Sarah feels this has strengthened her bond with her children, and she is not hesitant to tell anyone,

> *Ghost, guardian angel or a brief moment where I went a little crazy. Call it what you want, but to me it was my own ghost story, and I am happy for the experience. I look forward to what the future will reveal, in life and when the time comes....Following the death of my physical body, I have an old man who wears Brut cologne to track down and thank.*

"Instruct the wise and they will be wiser still; teach the righteous and they will add to their learning." —*Proverbs 9:9 NIV*

THE DOPPELGÄNGER

Karen worked at the Tippecanoe Mall in Lafayette for over two years and had nothing unusual happen. She was a graduate student at Purdue University, studying veterinary science. To her family and friends, she was always considered a go-to for support and help but also thought of as being overly serious. She certainly was not the sort to believe in the paranormal.

Karen was always a rule follower. When she was assigned a job to do, she would not stop until it was complete. During the Christmas season, things picked up at Macy's, where she worked, and she was often asked to pick up another shift. Between work and studying, she had no social life, so she did not mind the chance to earn some extra money.

One morning, Karen arrived before the store opened and started preparing for her day. She made small talk with a coworker, then walked

The Tippecanoe Mall is the largest mall in Lafayette. *W.C. Madden photo.*

out of the back room into what she believed was an empty store. Karen stopped in her tracks when she saw herself adjusting the clothes on a rack. The person was her exact duplicate. They made eye contact. This sent a chill up Karen's spine, and she let out a piercing scream. Her coworker ran out of the back and tried to comfort Karen, assuring her after a quick search that there was nobody else was in the store.

Karen resumed her workday with nothing out of the ordinary happening, but the frightening experience of seeing herself was branded in her mind. Over the next few days, Karen had an uneasy feeling like she was being watched whenever she arrived at work.

About four days later, she was working in the back room when a coworker came in, saw her and struggled to talk to her. The woman finally found her voice and told Karen, "I thought I just walked past you in the store."

"You must have seen my doppelgänger," Karen said.

"What's that?"

"A lookalike of me."

To some, seeing a doppelgänger is a bad omen, while others believe it is a warning. Seeing the doppelgänger really unnerved Karen, giving her butterflies in her stomach and leaving her with a sick feeling. Over the next month, Karen saw her doppelgänger two more times. Once, she glimpsed her doppelgänger standing behind her in the store mirror, and on the second occasion, she viewed herself walking into the back room. Each time, she was frightened, but she inwardly convinced herself that she had to ignore the visions.

Right before Christmas, a very handsome young man in his mid-twenties came into the store and started flirting with Karen. He asked her to go out with him after work. He told her he would pick her up in front of Macy's and described his car. After work, Karen felt full of excitement and anticipation. She had not gone out with anyone in a very long time. As she stepped outside of Macy's, she saw the young man's car. As she got closer, she saw him in the driver's side seat, waving her over. She started in that direction but stopped suddenly when she saw the doppelgänger in his passenger seat.

The young man apparently had not seen the doppelgänger, and he looked confused when Karen began to back up. She turned around and quickly headed back inside the mall, catching a glimpse of him getting out of his car in her peripheral vision. Without looking back, she walked through Macy's in the direction of the section where she worked. Her hands were shaking with fear. Entering the store, she walked past her coworkers and into the back room to catch her breath. A few minutes later, a coworker who had just started the day came looking for her. She told Karen that the man was there and asking for her but added,

I'm not trying to get in your business, but you should know I had a friend who went out with him a few years ago, and he beat her nearly to death while he was high on meth. He went to prison, I heard, but he must have just gotten out.

Karen left the back room and told the man she had made a mistake. She said she just didn't have time to go out with him. His early charm deserted him, and he yelled at her profanely. She quickly returned to the store. Karen was still feeling unnerved by the experience of seeing her doppelgänger and waited for a friend to get off work and walk with her out to her car.

As time passed, Karen began to view her experience with the doppelgänger differently. The image still unnerved her and gave her an eerie feeling; however, she now feels it was meant to save her from a bad decision. Since she decided not to go out with the charming, handsome customer, the apparition has never reappeared.

A HAUNTING AT LAFAYETTE JEFF

You might think a modern school wouldn't be haunted, but Jefferson High School is just that.

Jefferson High has a longstanding history in the Lafayette community. Located at 1801 South Eighteenth Street, Lafayette Jeff, as it's called, has a history of outstanding alumni ranging from doctors—such as George Robert Delong, who graduated in 1953 and went on to study medicine at Harvard—to musicians, including Donald Ambler, who graduated in 1947 and went on to play for the Chicago Civic Orchestra. Perhaps the most well-known local graduate of the former Lafayette Jeff was Bob Rohrman, who passed away on September 1, 2020, at age eighty-seven. Rohrman built an automobile empire across the city and the Midwest. The former graduate gave back to his former school by having the sensational Bob Rohrman Performing Arts Center built in 2009, which was made possible by his $3.5 million donation.

The school has an extensive history going back to the early 1900s and has been relocated and rebuilt in various locations to meet the needs of

Jefferson High School has a ghost story. *W.C. Madden photo.*

the growing community. The current school was built on a forty-three-acre section of historical land around the former Pythian Home on South Eighteenth and dedicated on May 24, 1970. Many have experienced memorable years achieving an education at the notable school. High school is an impactful time—for some a wonderful experience, but for others a social nightmare. Emotions are felt and coped with in different forms in the impressionable teen years. Not surprisingly, along with the successful area representative of the alumni, the school harbors spirits of the past.

The following account of paranormal activity was experienced by a current teacher. To avoid it becoming a distraction to her students, we will simply refer to her as Mrs. Jeff. She had an eerie encounter that left her a believer in what the rational mind can't process. When she first started teaching at the school, she noticed little oddities. Her keys, pen or other simple objects appeared to move from one place to the other without her recalling moving them. On other occasion, for several months, her pencil holder was turned over every morning when she came in, and her plastic utility cabinet drawer was open. At first, she was annoyed, thinking somehow a student did it as a prank or the janitorial staff was touching her things. She would ask, and no one fessed up to what she thought was a prank.

One afternoon, just after school got out and the rush of students leaving the halls had fallen silent, she was sitting at her desk reviewing her lesson plan for the next day. Suddenly, she heard a giggle just feet from where she sat. She looked up into the classroom, yet no one was there. She decided the sound must have traveled from the hall and continued her work. A few minutes later, a poster she had on the wall suddenly fell. As she stood up to retrieve it, she again heard a giggle from within the classroom. Since she was alone, she convinced her rational mind that it must have come from outside in the halls somewhere. She noticed that the room felt cold, so she calmly grabbed her belongings and decided to head for home.

The event played in her mind later that night, and she even shared it with her husband, who teased her a bit for suggesting there was a ghost in the school. She laughed at herself and put the notion to rest, since many students stayed after school for practices. She figured the giggle had to be an echo from one of the kids somewhere in the hallway.

The following week, her view on the paranormal was forever changed. It made her a defender of the idea that there are things we can't explain. As she was sitting at her desk reviewing students' work after school, she felt a cold draft. Grabbing her sweater, she walked outside the classroom to a faculty bathroom. As she walked, she felt an odd chill on the back of her neck. She explained it as someone taking an ice cube to her skin; this is how it felt to her. For a brief moment, she wondered if she was getting sick but dismissed the thought, as she was someone who seemed to never get ill.

Mrs. Jeff went into the restroom, and before leaving, she stepped up to the sink to wash her hands. Looking into the mirror, she suddenly froze. Standing directly behind her was the transparent image of a teenage girl with long pigtails and a starched, collared shirt from the 1970s era. Closing her eyes and gripping the sink, she felt her legs wobble and become weak. Although it was only seconds that had passed, she felt like it had been an eternity. Taking some deep breaths to steady herself, she inwardly gave herself a pep talk. Encouraging herself to open her eyes, she told herself it was her imagination. Taking one last deep breath, she opened her eyes and met her imagination in the mirror. Behind her was the bathroom and nothing else. Exhaling, she quickly turned to leave—and stopped in her tracks. Nearly nose to nose with her was the image that had been in the mirror a moment before. Only this time, the girl seemed as human as her and had piercing brown eyes filled with hostility.

Mrs. Jeff forced her body to respond, and she actually felt the teenage girl as a solid but icy being as she pushed passed her, stumbling into the hallway. Once in the hall, she fell against the wall, using it to hold her up as she made her way to a section of the school where students were standing in the hallway, preparing for band practice. Her heart was racing so hard she feared she would become an apparition herself as she struggled to steady herself. Mrs. Jeff watched some students practicing for band, using the time to settle her thoughts and also admitting to herself that she was too afraid to go back to her room for her keys. She considered making a mad escape from what was now her biggest fright.

After practice, Mrs. Jeff asked two of the students to come with her and assist her in taking some items to her vehicle that she could not carry herself. In truth, she needed an excuse to have an escort to retrieve her keys. Once she was settled in her vehicle, she still felt her hands shaking and had the eerie feeling she was being watched as she drove away.

During the next day and the weeks that followed, she opted to use a student restroom during passing periods to make sure she would not be alone. She did everything she could to ensure she was never alone, not even in her own classroom. She admitted little oddities still occurred, but she ignored them, and in the years since her ghostly encounter in the bathroom, she has not seen the teenage girl with the long pigtails and angry eyes.

SITTING AROUND THE CAMPFIRE TELLING GHOST STORIES

The lure of gathering in the outdoors to sit around an evening bonfire while camping brings thousands to Indiana-area campgrounds each year. Part of the thrill of camping is the nighttime tales of horror and fright told around the campfire. To some, it is a tradition nestled in the idea of making fun memories with family and friends, but to others, the reality of experiencing real haunts and spooks while camping will forever keep them away from the campfire ritual.

Just outside Lafayette is the small community of Americus, with a population of only 423, according to the 2010 census. The community is considered part of the Lafayette metropolitan statistical area, yet it's a quiet and rural area with homes spread out across fields of corn and wooded areas running along the Wabash River. Located on Old State Road 25 North in this area is the quaint and welcoming Wolfe's Leisure Time Campground.

This is the old broken-down bus in Wolfe's Leisure Time Campground. *Dorothy Salvo Benson photo.*

The destination is an anticipated retreat for the many returning seasonal campers who enjoy the atmosphere of days gone by with the kind of hospitality given by owners Dale and Mary Wolfe. The location has forty acres holding two playgrounds, a basketball court, a game and recreation room, concessions, fishing and hiking and biking trails, to name just some of the fun and easily available activities.

This is a golf-cart-friendly campground, and on any given day, passersby wave to each other and join together for weekly events hosted by the owners. The location is picture perfect and ideal to set the scene for any inspirational or romantic film. The campground has another interesting focal point that has become part of its history and led to several myths and ghostly tales regarding where it originated. Among the campground trails, you will find a path winding alongside the Wabash River, leading to an old bus sunk into the mud, rusting and daring you to guess how it was left behind.

In good fun, the owners created their own spooky tale that can be found on their Facebook page but admit it was just in the spirit of Halloween and holds no truth. What might surprise even them is that there may be some truth to a haunting that is connected to that old bus so many have come to love and embrace as part of the campground's nostalgic charm.

In the summer of 2018, Cathy Thomas from Illinois had come to stay with family in their RV for a weekend retreat at the campground. Thomas is a schoolteacher nearing retirement and considers herself to be "of a rational mind"; she has always been described by those who know her as serious. Living alone since her husband's passing a few years back, she never has been easily spooked, nor has she given in to letting her imagination get the best of her. Her ability to stay calm and think rationally came to be a great asset early one evening as she walked alongside the river's path at Wolfe's campground.

As she walked alone, Cathy took in the natural beauty of the sun shining through the trees, seeing the broken-down old school bus up ahead. She still recalls thinking to herself how unique the scene before her looked. "It had a stillness that was not creepy but calming and reminded me of times from my own childhood when moments just seemed to be so much bigger than they actually were," she said.

As she approached the bus, Cathy heard the sudden sound of whimpering. Stopping alongside the bus, she listened to the sound and was not sure where it was coming from. Her rational mind began to consider the possibilities, telling herself that sometimes animals crying can sound like small children.

Looking around the bus and glancing at the woods around her, she saw no sign of where the sound was coming from. An odd sensation traveled up her spine, and the hair rose on her arms, but she said that she was not feeling afraid, just confused. Cathy explained,

> *I remember thinking to myself, I must be experiencing what people have referred to as a sixth sense; something was unusual, more than just the sound. There was a feeling in the air around me that I don't have a way to describe, but still I was not afraid. Can't say why I wasn't, other than this sense of calm that was surrounding me.*

When Cathy turned to walk back the way she had come, she suddenly felt a small hand take hers. She looked down, and big brown eyes stared back up at her. Holding her hand was a small child with tears in his eyes, looking desperately at her. The boy was wearing swim trucks that looked vintage and brown sandals. His hair was cut in an out-of-date bowl-style way that she had not seen since her own childhood. She asked him if he was lost and where his parents were. The small boy took some deep breaths while still crying softly and tugged on her hand. Cathy let him lead her back to the opening of the bus, where a door once was. He pointed for her to step inside the bus, which she pointed out was unsafe; she encouraged him to go back with her to the campsites to find his parents. Cathy gently tugged the boy's hand to pull him away from the door and toward the path, when suddenly, her hand felt free. The boy had disappeared. She felt a cool breeze blow past her and confesses that her knees became shaky with a feeling of fright and confusion. The calm feeling escaped her, and her mind struggled to decide on her next move: fight or flight? When the boy reappeared as an obvious apparition, standing inside the bus before her, floating slightly above the ground, transparent and grinning as he waved her to come forward, her instinct for flight took over, and she ran back to the path and kept running back to her family's campsite.

When Cathy returned to her campsite, her family was off enjoying other activities. She sat for some time outside the RV, in sight of other campers, trying to collect herself and consider what she had just seen. By the time her family returned about half an hour later, she was still shaking but feeling more composed and able to share her encounter.

As Cathy told her family what she had experienced, she surprised herself when she felt that she knew the spirit meant her no harm. "I can't say why, really, but I get the feeling he was just lonely and wanted someone to play with," she said as she reflected on the encounter. "I don't think he was trying to scare me at all." Despite this revelation, she admits she did feel a little nervous going to sleep that night. Having enjoyed the campground so much, she stayed but did not venture toward the bus on her last day.

Cathy's family still enjoys this campground, and she admits she can see why. "It really is a great place to stay," she shares. "There is a real sense of community there. Makes sense to me now why a spirit would choose that location to occupy. You feel like you're with family, even when reality is all strangers gathering for weekend fun."

Over the years, some have speculated that the bus fell into the river and all the passengers inside perished. Others have created a myth that it broke down and the frustrated bus driver threw each child into the river, drowning them. According to the owners, the bus broke down just where it sits today on March 1, 1997. Although they don't know how it came to rest in the location, they do know it was converted from a bus to a camper at one point, based on how it was when they first saw it. They have no idea why someone may have lived in it as a camper or who they were. They do not know if it broke down while being used as a camper and was deserted. At the present time, it has been gutted and is simply the remains of an old bus.

Dale Wolfe hopes to "give people the experience of an old-fashioned campground with modern amenities." Considering how many campers return, it is fair to say the Wolfes have achieved their goal of giving visitors the positive impression of past and present coming together.

WALDRON-BECK HOUSE

The following story was nearly left out of this book when accounts of paranormal sightings were first being gathered. Initially, reports were of your classic ghostly sightings that did not amount to much to write an entire story about. The claims came in from those passing by North Twenty-First Street in Lafayette. People insisted they had seen a middle-aged woman dressed in attire from the mid- to late-1800s along the side of the road. Then an email was received from a woman who passes by Swan Dermatology & Aesthetics daily on her way to work; she claimed to have seen the woman several times over the years, dismissing it each time until the day she saw the woman disappear right in front of her.

Sara Freemont, a health care worker, explained,

I was driving when suddenly the woman stepped into the street right in front of my car! She was coming from the opposite side of where Swan Dermatology & Aesthetics is located. I knew I could not avoid her and hit my brakes! The car would have hit her in her long full skirt and knocked the hat right off her head, except that she disappeared right before my eyes!

That incident occurred in the spring of 2021, and Sara now takes a different route to work in an effort to avoid another encounter with the ghostly apparition. This encounter was interesting, but not enough to get it into the pages of this book—until a social media message came in from Stephanie Johnson, sharing her encounter with what appeared to be the same ghostly female apparition. Johnson was going through a difficult divorce and struggling to manage her emotions. She drove her sister to an appointment at Swan Dermatology & Aesthetics and was waiting outside one fateful afternoon. Her sister had encouraged her to make an appointment herself, telling her that the facial she got did more than help her look better; the care she received was mentally uplifting and therapeutic. Struggling to get out of her depression, Johnson agreed to drive her sister to the appointment and wait outside. Johnson reflected back and began having unhealthy thoughts, missing her ex-husband. Her hands began to shake, and she got out of her car to have a cigarette.

It was a nice sunny day, and Johnson walked toward the road as she inhaled the nicotine, trying to calm her nerves. Just as Johnson got to the street and was turning to walk back toward her car, she felt a hand on her shoulder. She turned to her left, and there stood a fully flesh-and-blood woman wearing period clothing from the 1800s. It was an odd moment. Johnson took a step back as the woman passed by her, walking toward the Swan's Dermatology building. The woman in the long, dark burgundy dress paused and looked back at Johnson, motioning for her to follow. Unable to stop herself, Johnson walked behind the woman toward the building. She heard her sister call out to her. Johnson turned her head, only for a second, to look in the direction of her sister, but when she looked back, the strangely dressed woman was gone.

Johnson asked her sister where the woman had gone. Her sister had no idea what she was talking about. She claimed to have seen no one walking in front of Johnson. This should have unnerved the recently divorced woman, who had been living on the brink of tears for weeks, but it had just the opposite effect. Johnson can't explain it, but following the encounter, she felt renewed with a sense of motivation, looking ahead instead of behind. This feeling began immediately after her encounter with the woman she later believed to be an apparition.

That was certainly an enticing paranormal experience worth writing about, but it became more significant when the next message came in about an experience another woman had with a ghostly woman inside the Swan Dermatology & Aesthetics building.

For the sake of her privacy, we will call this woman Kate. She had also been having some personal struggles with her own relationship. Her boyfriend of seven years cheated on her at a friend's bachelor party. He came clean himself and confessed it to her, blaming it on alcohol and poor judgment. He also knew that her brother had found out and would likely tell her. This was not the first time he had made this mistake over the years, but once again, he made her feel guilty for being angry, and she said she would forgive him. They were working through it, but Kate was blaming herself. She went to Swan's because she always left feeling better, like Johnson's sister, who claimed the service she was provided improved not only her outward appearance but also her mental health.

Following Kate's appointment at the office, she stopped in the restroom before leaving. As she looked at herself in the mirror, she was feeling good but had nagging thoughts, wondering if her boyfriend was still thinking about the one-night stand he had. She also asked herself why she did not have the strength to move past him to someone who would treat her better. As she looked in the mirror, she suddenly saw the image of a woman dressed in full 1800s attire, with hat included, standing behind her. Kate was frozen where she stood but could not look away. Her heart began to race, and her knees grew weak, but this lasted only a moment before an odd calm came over her. As she looked at the woman, they held eye contact. The woman's lips never moved, but Kate heard her say, "It is a bottom fact, he will tell more thumpers." The woman reached out and touched Kate's shoulder before fading away.

Kate stood for a moment longer without turning around and just stared at her own reflection. She felt instantly empowered and calm in a way she had never before experienced. She thought of the woman as she drove home and did not try to dismiss the experience as an illusion. She was confident in what she saw and, more importantly, the experience triggered a motivation to move on to the next chapter in her life.

That night, Kate ended the relationship with her cheating boyfriend and has since found herself in a healthy and loving relationship. A few weeks following the experience, the ghostly words repeated in her mind. At the time, she was unsure of their meaning, but after a little research, Kate learned that in the 1800s, a common way of saying someone was lying was to say they were telling "thumpers." The words made sense to her now, and she felt certain she had made the right choice by moving on. Her ghostly encounter happened a few years back but has greatly affected the direction her life went. Kate now lives in southern Indiana and does not refer to the woman she saw staring back at her in the mirror as a ghost; instead, she calls her a guardian of women.

Kate's final view of the woman could be viewed as merely a nice sentiment, a way of remembering a situation that helped a woman move past an unhealthy relationship, and be left out of the story, if not for the fascinating connection this apparition or "guardian of women" has with that particular area. There is a historic home directly across the street from Swan Dermatology & Aesthetics called the Waldron-Beck and Carriage House. The home was built in 1877–78 for Edward H. Waldron and his wife, Mary Russell (Beauchamp) Waldron. Edward was a successful member of the community, and the couple married in September 1865. In 1875, the couple relocated for a short period to St. Louis but returned to Lafayette in 1877, living in the home as husband and wife until 1886. In 1886, Waldron abandoned his wife, relocating to Chicago. After a business acquaintance died in February 1886, Waldron is believed to have started an affair with his widow. Feeling embarrassment, mental anguish and shame because of the actions of her husband, Mary filed for divorce, and the petition was granted in June 1887. In October 1887, E.H. Waldron married Josephine P. Alexander, the widow his ex-wife suspected him of having an affair with. Mary Russell was clearly a strong woman for her time, and she did not take the actions of her husband easily. He and his new wife had shamed her, so she decided they should pay for what they did. In June 1888, Mary Russell, the former Mrs. Waldron, sued Mrs. Josephine P. Waldron on the grounds that her involvement with her former husband while they were married wrongfully and wickedly injured the plaintiff. The suit went to trial, and Russell sought out justice for the hurt and harm her former husband's affair caused her.

This perhaps explains why the apparition is seen coming from what would have been the home of Mary Russell Beauchamp (formerly Waldron). Could it be that she finds comfort in helping those who are in need of uplifting?

It could be said that she appreciates businesses like Swan's Dermatology that seek to empower people to feel at their best. Undeniably, there is an interesting connection between Mary Russell Beauchamp's situation and the life situations these women were experiencing at the time they had personal encounters with her.

CHAPTER 16
TIPTON COUNTY

OLD FACTORY HAUNTED

An old factory in Sharpsville is haunted, according to the Will County Ghost Hunters Society.

The old factory has been closed down for years, but it seems some other activity is occurring there. People have reported hearing people talking and metal clanging in the factory when no one is inside.

CHAPTER 17
WABASH COUNTY

HAUNTED GRAVEL PIT IN DISKO

The gravel pit near Disko reportedly has had an apparition of a woman dressed in purple tattered clothing, according to the Will County Ghost Hunters Society. The identity of this woman is not known. Why she is there is also unknown. Many local residents have seen her. Disko is an unincorporated community.

The haunted gravel pit in Disko is owned by Speedway Sand & Gravel. *W.C. Madden photo.*

WABASH COUNTY STATE FOREST

Some strange things have occurred in the Wabash County State Forest.

People have reported having periods of time unaccounted for. People have seen balls of light that seem to dart around them, as if they were being watched. Some shadowy figures have been seen running through the woods. Also, the smell of death has been perceived on numerous occasions.

CHAPTER 18

WARREN COUNTY

THREE FIRES, YOU'RE OUT!

You would think that there's something wrong at a site where three buildings burned down over the years. Was it fate, or was the site haunted?

The first structure built at the site in Warren County near Williamsport was the Mudlavia Hotel. Originally called Indiana Springs Company, the hotel was built in 1880 by Harry Lewis Kramer, a twenty-nine-year-old entrepreneur who lived in Attica in Fountain County. He attracted investors and started up a health resort at a spot near the spectacular Fall Creek Gorge in neighboring Warren County. He built the hotel at the site of a natural spring because of a Civil War veteran named Samuel Story, who claimed the spring had healing properties. A sufferer of rheumatism himself, Story claimed his symptoms disappeared after he drank the natural spring water he discovered in 1884 while he was digging a drainage ditch. The hotel drew many of the wealthy and famous to its grounds for the spring's supposed healing properties. Famous Indiana author James Whitcomb Riley was a guest at the hotel. The hotel claimed to heal and alleviate a large number of various diseases and maladies. Rumor has it that several famous gangsters even visited the hotel, including John Dillinger and Al Capone.

The hotel thrived and became known nationwide, drawing people from all over the country to the small rural community, until fire broke out on February 29, 1920, and destroyed the main building. The hotel ceased operations, but this did not stop people from coming out to the property. Many spiritual and, some say, demonic rituals were held on the grounds.

Later, a smaller building containing a restaurant called Pleasant Valley Lodge was constructed. It burned down in 1968. After Pleasant Valley closed, another owner returned the building to its original name of Mudlavia Lodge until it, too, burned down in 1974.

Many believe that the rituals held on the property have released a negative or demonic presence that remains on the grounds and seeks to overtake and destroy any presence that enters.

Catherine Little was a nineteen-year-old teenager in the 1990s when she went to visit the remains of the second structure that burned down where the grand hotel once stood. Her friends brought along an old wooden Ouija board and a case of beer, intending to have some fun calling out to the spirits. Little reveals she really had no intention of trying to communicate with the dead, nor did she even believe in it as a possibility. She was more motivated by a teenage crush she had on another member of the group.

Little confessed to trespassing onto the grounds, which she did not realize she was doing until they were chased off later on. When she first arrived, it was already getting dark, and the group pulled out their flashlights as they entered the ruins.

The first thing Little noticed was the graffiti that was scribbled across all the walls. It became clear to her that others came out to the location for mischief, and that is when she began to feel nervous and started having second thoughts about being there. The group found a spot near an old fireplace to set up their board and then lit some candles. Many in the group laughed and enjoyed good-humored banter while they tried to scare each other as they shared in a few beers before starting their séance.

The group of seven teens sat in a circle and joined hands while they began to call out to the spirits. The time was about nine at night, and Little admits she felt a little ridiculous when they would pause to listen for a disembodied voice to suddenly answer them. They never got a response or any movement on the board, and the group was about to leave when suddenly they all experienced what Little can only describe as a blackout.

Little can only share her own experience but makes a point of emphasizing that everyone in the group had their own personal "episode" that night. Little described what happened to her by calling it a flashback. A few years before, she talked a group of friends into joining her in cornering and beating up a girl she was very jealous of. To get them to join her in the attack, Little admits she lied and created rumors about the girl. In her flashback, she was brought back to the day, but not as herself. She was inside of the girl she had attacked and felt every ounce of the fear and pain the girl experienced.

Little described her experience as the most emotional and painful thing she has ever gone through. Panic rose in her when she was suddenly jolted "awake" while sitting in the circle with her friends on the grounds of the old Mudlavia Hotel. At the exact moment Little was brought back, she squealed in terror and noted everyone else in the circle had the same response at the exact same time. They all quickly stood and started to run toward their vehicles when they were met by headlights. To this day, Little is not sure who they were, but a woman and man in their thirties jumped out of their car and yelled at them to get off the property before they called the police. The group of teens did not hesitate; they immediately left the property. As they drove away, they still had not shared their experiences. One of the others in the car with Little pointed out it was after two in the morning. They had totally lost track of time, and Little was anxious to get as far from Mudlavia as she could.

The next night, the group met at a Denny's, and as talk began, they discovered that each one of them had been brought back to an event in their past when they hurt someone. Each had experienced it from the point of view of the person they harmed and felt the pain they caused.

Little can't explain what happened to her that night, and she still does not know if she believes in ghosts, but she does believe in paranormal, unexplained events. Regarding whether she believes Mudlavia has true healing powers, Little says she doesn't know if it can cure physical ailments, but she does believe it can straighten out someone's behavior.

CHAPTER 19

WHITE COUNTY

THE GIRL OF GHOST HOLLOW

During the summer of 2007, a city worker was finishing up some work on North Main Street in Monticello, the county seat, when he caught a glimpse of something he will always remember.

Ghost Hollow is located on North Main Street in Monticello. *W.C. Madden photo.*

The road was being widened, and the bridge that went over Ghost Hollow Creek was being redone to accommodate the new road. This project was a much-needed improvement to the growing city, but despite the change to the present, the past remains.

About seven o'clock, after a long day in the sun, thoughts of a sandwich and a cold drink were inspiring this city worker to gather his items in haste. As he rushed, his pocketknife fell out of his pocket. Mumbling his frustration, he climbed down from where he was working on the road above into the ravine below to retrieve the knife. As he reached the spot where his knife had fallen, he heard a horse's soft neighing and looked in the direction of the sound. In the distance, he was stunned to see the silhouette of a woman on a horse. Although it was just a shadow, the rider's skirt made it apparent to him that it was indeed a lady. As the moment passed, the pair, horse and rider, blended into the shadows beyond. Just like that, they were gone. Recovering from his shock, the worker went home that day in wonder at what he saw.

Ray, a local old-timer, claims that when he was a boy, he was told never to play near the creek. He heard a legend that, in the 1800s, a young woman was crossing that area on horseback when she fell and hit her head, dying instantly.

Two local residents live by the area and have lighted signs on each side of the entrance to their shared driveway. They say "Ghost Hollow."

Did this tragic accident happen? One can only speculate. If you run into the woman on horseback, perhaps she can give you an answer to the question, if you dare to ask.

SPOOKY INDIANA BEACH

Indiana Beach is an amusement park located near Monticello that has been around since 1926. It now celebrates Halloween by decorating the park in September and staying open until the annual celebration. There is one place in the park that is haunted, according to a couple of people.

The old Terrainescope Observatory (*left*) is haunted. *W.C. Madden photo.*

Vendor Jennifer Ousley has a food outlet and store on Paradise Island in the old Terrainescope Observatory building that was constructed in the 1950s. She uses the old observatory for storage, since it is no longer used for observing. She's heard strange sounds coming from the observatory.

One day, she took another vendor, Charlotte Reed, up to the observatory after they heard some knocking. "I do feel energy there," said Reed. "Upstairs is really heavy." Reed says she is a medium.

THE ACTIVE SOLDIER

On a late May afternoon, a couple of friends, Sue and Joanne, were taking a walk on Prairie Street in Brookston, an ideal, picture-perfect town in southern White County.

As the young women were power walking, they were enjoying a lively conversation. Sue asked Joanne a question. When she didn't receive a response, she turned to look at her friend. Seeing a puzzled look on Joanne's face, she asked, "Joanne, did you hear me?"

Staring straight ahead, Joanne responded, "Do you see that man coming towards us?"

Prairie Street is a main street in Brookston that runs south to north through downtown. *W.C. Madden photo.*

Sue looked in the direction of Joanne and stopped. Heading directly toward the girls was a young man in what looked like a Civil War uniform. He wore a blue coat and pants. He had a belt with a sword hanging from his waist and a blue kepi cap.

What made the girls most uncomfortable was the bayonet attached to the rifle. He carried the rifle on his shoulder as he walked at a quick, determined pace.

Just as Joanne was about to ask Sue if there was some Civil War reenactment in the area, the man, who was only about fifteen feet away, suddenly looked at them. It was only a brief moment, and then he vanished. The women were stunned.

Once the shock and confusion gave way to the reality of what the women had just encountered, they were both very frightened. For the first time, their power walk turned into a run as they headed home.

Although the women no longer walk along Prairie Street, as they prefer the treadmills at a nearby gym, both are convinced the man they saw was indeed a Union soldier.

Perhaps he's searching for the family he left behind well over a century ago when he went off to war. One can only wonder.

THE PACING MAN

Judy had been married to the only man she ever loved since she was sixteen. They were raising two children. Her life was stable and content.

In 1959, she was a young mother with two children, ages one and two, who were usually on each hip at the time. The family lived in Idaville, but Judy often spent her days taking care of her grandmother, who was not well and lived in Burnettsville. She took walks with her young children during the day while her grandmother napped.

On one walk at about eleven-thirty in the morning one day, as she was walking past the Burnettsville First Baptist Church, she noticed a man frantically pacing back and forth. He seemed not to take notice of them. Judy hurried on by, because she thought it was odd and she felt a strange sympathy for him.

After returning home that evening, Judy shared the story with her husband. He thought she was making much about nothing, and he had little to say. Judy put the matter out of her mind in a few days. When she returned to

First Baptist Church is located in Burnettsville. *W.C. Madden photo.*

her grandmother's house, she again took a walk with the children while her grandmother napped. To her surprise, as Judy passed the church, the man was there again, pacing back and forth. This time, she realized his clothes were all wet, despite the nice, dry day. She thought about saying something, but she took her husband's advice and minded her own business.

Over the next week, at the same time of day, every time Judy took her walk, she saw the pacing man, just as before. It was not until the fourth time that she realized he had the same clothes on each time, and they always seemed wet.

Judy pleaded with her husband that night to meet her for her walk the next day to see this strange man and maybe talk to him. Her husband felt like she was being a busybody and exaggerating the event. He refused.

The next day, Judy decided to go on her walk alone, but she had to wait for a neighbor to watch the children. By this time, it was late afternoon, and as she passed the church, the man was not there.

Frustrated with herself, she went home and tried to put the man out of her mind. Yet she found her train of thought again returning to the man. She wondered why he kept walking back and forth with the same wet clothes on at about the same time. And why did he never even notice her? She was consumed with thoughts of the strange man, and whenever she talked about him to someone else, they didn't seem interested.

On Monday the next week, Judy went on the walk with her children. Sure enough, the man was walking. Judy decided she was going to find out what he was doing there. Slowly, she walked up to him with one child on her hip and the other holding her hand. Judy walked up behind him, and as he turned around suddenly to face her, he passed right through her and the children. Judy was stunned. She turned around to confront him, and he was gone. She returned to her grandmother's house and was hysterical. Judy convinced her grandmother to watch the children. Then she ran next door to get a neighbor to seek out the man. Her search for help only ended up with her making a fool out of herself.

Judy's grandmother called Judy's husband, and he came to her house. He took his shocked wife and the children home. He was angry and embarrassed by his wife's behavior. He forbade her to take walks in that direction. As the years passed, Judy didn't talk about the man she saw, but she never let the experience leave her memory.

Back in 1859, a tornado hit Burnettsville and destroyed a church as it was nearing completion. A house was also demolished. There were no deaths, however. Interestingly, the event occurred one hundred years before Judy's experience with the man—or was it a ghost?

THE DARK MAN

Ever get the feeling that maybe you're not alone? Ever have a sixth sense that makes you feel like someone is standing at the foot of your bed? Only when you open your eyes, except for an eerie feeling, you find nothing.

Well, Dave and Jody were not so fortunate. Just six miles south of Monticello by Springboro and Big Creek stands a home that was originally a two-car garage. After the conversion of the garage into a home was complete, the couple began to experience strange things. It was as if the ground beneath the house had been awakened from a restful slumber.

The couple had been together for twenty years, although to look at Jody, you would not think she was old enough. They were total opposites in every possible way, except for the love reflected in their eyes. Jody is easy to talk to and very open. She is a woman who's very aware of the idea there is more out there than what we see.

Now, Dave is just the opposite. He is an excellent worker and will accomplish anything he puts his mind to. He will finish all things he starts. He has a strong mind and isn't open to the idea of the paranormal like his wife seems to be.

As Dave stood by Jody's side, listening to her story, he was not yet ready to voice out loud what he saw. Jody stated that not long after the construction was complete, she started to feel a presence in the home—not a friendly presence, either. The smell of tobacco smoke and lavender or lilac perfume would drift through the house. Sometimes sounds of someone else in the home could be heard. Jody would enter a room and immediately get the feeling she was invading someone's space. Whenever she would mention these events to her husband, he would dismiss them. That is, until he had his own encounters.

One evening, as the couple slept, they both woke to the feeling there was someone in the room. Dave opened his eyes, looked toward the doorway and saw the dark form of a tall man in a suit and hat. It was very dark, and the man's face could not be distinguished. Dave received a very cold and unwanted feeling from the dark figure. Their sleep was disturbed a few more times, and although Jody never looked toward the door, she never doubted her husband, as she also experienced the strong feeling the entity spawned.

Dave was determined to deny to himself what he was seeing, so he kept trying to create excuses, but one night, when the dark figure began to walk toward him, that was enough. He jumped up, threw his pillow at the spirit and screamed at it, "Leave me alone!"

The spirit disappeared, but its presence stayed and never allowed the couple to find peace in their home. That was enough for the couple. Not long after that confrontation with the dark figure, the couple moved.

Dennis Krintz and his son Chad look for artifacts after Lake Freeman was lowered in 1993. *Photo provided by Dennis Krintz.*

What was interesting was the discovery made nearby not long after they left. When Lake Freeman was lowered in 1993, remains of Native Americans were discovered by Dennis Krintz and archaeologists from Purdue University during a dig. Could this be connected to the couple's unwelcome visitor?

LATE ARRIVAL

On a fall afternoon in 2005, Juan R. was traveling from his job outside of Reynolds to his home in Monon. It was about six o'clock, and the sky was growing dark as evening approached. The air outside was growing cold, so he rolled up his car windows. As he approached the old train, a woman in a turn-of-the-century dress caught his eye. She seemed to be disembarking off the side of a passenger car of the steam engine train.

Thinking it odd and not sure he saw the lady correctly, Juan continued to keep his eyes on the road. Suddenly, a moment later, he saw a woman on the side of the road just ahead. Juan quickly pulled over, not even sure to this day why. He explained that he felt compelled to do so. Once he pulled over, he looked out the window in front of him, and there stood the lady, with a carpetbag in her arms, looking straight at him. The woman was petite, with brown hair pulled tightly back from her face. She seemed to be in her mid-thirties. Juan thought she looked like the same woman he caught a glimpse of by the engine, but he knew that couldn't be possible. The detail he remembers the most is the woman's eyes. He claims to have never read so much confusion and sadness on someone's face as clearly as what he saw at that moment. His heart ached for her.

Just as Juan was about to get out of the car and speak with the woman, she faded away before his very eyes. What was only a matter of seconds seemed to happen in slow motion as her eyes held his until she was gone. Juan thinks of the sad woman by the road every day. He has even found himself praying for her to have found peace. What the woman was trying to tell him about this life, he may never know, but through her sadness, he has strived to bring more joy to those he knows.

"May you never confront eyes so full of pain, because they will haunt you," he explained.

A TOWN ON FIRE

Casey was playing with her daughter, a very active two-year-old, at the Reynolds playground on a fall day. After getting home and preparing herself for company later that evening, she had thought it best to take her little one out of the house for a while.

Having a good hour to kill before her guest arrived, Casey was enjoying the bonding time with her daughter as they chased a butterfly. Suddenly, the odor of smoke filled the air. She stopped playing and searched the area around her. Finding nothing and thinking someone might be burning leaves, she resumed the chase with her daughter.

After a few minutes, the smell was so strong that Casey was getting a headache. Thinking it best to head for home, she picked up her daughter and placed her in the stroller. As she was leaving the park, she saw what looked like a large smoke cloud. It was as if the town was on fire. The smell of wood burning was obvious. Walking faster in the direction of the fire, she was shocked to find no cause for it. The scent suddenly vanished, and the smoke cloud was gone.

Casey describes the experience as frustrating, because she felt as if she was losing her mind. Over the years, she claims to have encountered two other people who have had similar experiences. Casey found some comfort when she shared the story with her grandmother, who told Casey that in the early 1800s, the town of Reynolds burned to the ground.

Casey's grandmother was partially right. The fire in downtown Reynolds occurred on August 21, 1907, and burned down a block of wood-frame buildings. Businesses that burned down included a post office, hardware store, barber shop, saloon, shoe store, restaurant, grocery, furniture store, blacksmith shop, Knights of Pythias Lodge, barn, telephone exchange and a residence.

THE CIVIL WAR SWORD

The Civil War broke the hearts of many White County residents. Perhaps it is the great emotion that was felt at this time in our great country's past that has led so many to turn this tragic event into a romantic story. It is of little surprise that paranormal events have followed the tragedy of the War Between the States.

A home in Chalmers on North First Street could hold a mystery that has yet to be solved. In the 1950s, Mr. and Mrs. Dawson were newlyweds and thrilled to be starting their lives together. Mrs. Dawson's uncle had generously allowed them to reside in his home, as he was currently living elsewhere.

Very early on their second morning in the home, the Dawsons were awakened by the sound of soft sobbing. It seemed to be coming from the yard outside. Mr. Dawson went out to investigate, and the sobbing stopped. He could not find the source and returned to bed.

This was on a Monday and quickly forgotten by the couple as they settled into the weekly routine. Then, exactly a month later at four in the morning, they were again awoken by the same sound of soft sobbing. Once again, when Mr. Dawson went out in the yard to investigate, he could find nothing, and the noise stopped.

This happened several more times over the next year. It always took place on a Monday at four in the morning and seemed to last only a few minutes.

That was the only strange occurrence on the property that the couple noticed, until one evening in July at about eleven, when Mr. Dawson could not sleep and went outside for some cool air. As he went out in the yard, he froze in his tracks. Before him was the image of a woman in a full skirt from the Civil War era and a man. He could not make out them out clearly. The man was more of a shadow, with his head being held by the woman as he lay in her lap. Mr. Dawson blinked several times, thinking his eyes were playing tricks on him, but the image did not vanish. He claims it lasted at least a full minute before suddenly disappearing. The man and woman never seemed aware of his presence.

Mr. Dawson returned inside and shared the experience with his wife, who then revealed to him that she saw a woman in the yard fitting the same description a few weeks earlier. She told him that she had quickly dismissed it, as it was out of the corner of her eye and she couldn't be certain of what she saw.

Over the next few months, other than the sobbing, which they had become used to, nothing happened.

One afternoon the following spring, a neighbor came over with his dog. The dog seemed to sense something in the exact spot Mr. Dawson had seen the image. The dog barked and attempted to dig in the area so intently that his owner apologized and took him home.

Later that spring, as the couple worked together to till the ground for a garden, they made an exciting discovery. In the ground exactly where the ghostly couple had been spotted, they found a Civil War sword. The blade was facing down with the handle up. It was a typical custom to put the sword in the ground this way at the spot where a soldier had died.

Could a soldier have made it home to his love before passing, or was the man who carried this sword a deserter who was in need of help but never made it home?

The couple claimed their garden at the location produced the best vegetation of any garden they have had since. The Dawsons lived in the home for another two years and claim to have never experienced anything else, except for the occasional sobbing, always on a Monday at four in the morning.

LAKEVIEW HOME WAS HAUNTED

In 1907, White County officials voted to construct a new county infirmary. It was known as the White County Asylum, and people called it the Poor Farm, as it housed people who didn't have the finances to live elsewhere. It was a good place for the homeless. Back then, all counties had such facilities, and some had insane asylums as well as juvenile asylums. This facility did have jail cells in the basement, and they were used when necessary. One time there was a murder in the facility as well.

This photo shows the old Lakeview Home being torn down in 2017. *W.C. Madden photo.*

Fast-forward to the future, and the asylum became the Lakeview Home. It was still a place for people who lacked money. In the mid-1990s, Deven Seward went to work there as a cleaning lady. She found it was haunted.

"One room in particular on the second floor was haunted," Seward explained. "When we would clean that room, if you didn't turn the light on, the door would slam behind us. And in the kitchen, you could see shadows and hear pans moving around at night."

In the wine cellar, they found broken bottles every time they went down there. "There was no way they'd fall off the racks," Deven said. They had to clean up the mess, of course.

One time, Deven looked down the laundry chute and swears she saw someone in the basement. "It was creepy," she said.

Her mother would never get out of the car when she dropped off Deven, as she didn't like the place and wouldn't go inside.

In 2010, White County officials decided to sell off the old home, as they no longer wanted to pay the overhead of the losing proposition. A company from Chicago purchased it and decided in 2017 to tear it down.

Seward was there only a short time, but she loved "the castle," as she called it. "So sad to see it torn down," she said.

SCARY FACTORY IN WOLCOTT

Dwyer Instruments is located at 204 West Sherry Lane in Wolcott. The factory was founded in 1931 and primarily manufactures pressure gauges. It has employed many residents from the community over the years. For those who live nearby, it offers a local place to work without the need to travel far from the small town. One of the employees was Mike, who worked at the factory for several years and recalls having really enjoyed his time there. "I worked there for years, and believe me, I didn't stay for the pay," he explained. "It was my coworkers—really good people."

Mike looks back at his time at the factory with fond memories, but it was also a time in his life when he experienced his own paranormal encounters there. He explained that the factory itself had an eerie feel to it. He could never really say why, though. The company actually kept it clean, as far as factories go. They even hired outside companies to send people in to clean up the break room, offices and bathrooms. The eerie feeling he got was not so much from the environment itself but the sensation that someone was watching him.

Mike clarified,

The first time I thought my mind was playing tricks on me was when I went into the break room to put my lunch in the fridge. We were supposed to put our names on things, but I had forgotten. I heard a voice behind me ask me where my name was. I figured it was a coworker, but I turned around and no one was there. I actually felt the hair stand up on the back of my neck.

Mike expounded that the break room was a good size, and it was not likely someone said it from outside the door, because the voice came from right behind where he stood. He convinced himself that he was hearing things and tried to brush it off as he went back to work. On another occasion, Mike shared that he once saw a solid black outline of a man in shadow move right through machinery and into a wall. He blinked several times, thinking his eyes were messing with him. Mike looked around; no one else seemed to have noticed, so he kept it to himself and went back to work.

Mike's worst experience was when he was in the men's room. He reflected back, taking a deep breath and pausing before he began again:

Now I know you're going to think I'm making this up, but I'm going to tell you anyway because I know what happened. I heard a voice when I was washing my hands. It was muffled and I could not make it out. It unnerved me, but I thought it was coming from outside the room. I turned the water off and that's when it happened. A male said my name, clear as day, and I felt someone flick my ear. A rush of adrenaline went through me, and I bolted for the door. I couldn't get it opened. Honestly, it felt like someone was holding it shut. I finally got it opened and was shaking when I left. I was just too embarrassed to tell anyone, but my hands kept shaking, and I went home claiming I was ill. I guess I was kinda ill after that.

Mike returned to work the next day and said nothing about what happened for a while. He would still get a spooky feeling that he was being watched and feel unexplained, cold rushes of air. The most difficult thing that came from his experience was feeling like he could not share it.

Mike continued,

I noticed right away that [my coworker] *Sue looked pale and seemed to be shaking. She just came in and sat down fidgeting with her hands and staying nothing. This was not like her at all. She was one of the sweetest ladies you could meet and always chatted away. I asked her if she was okay, and she then shared with me what happened to her. It was almost the exact same thing as what happened to me.*

Mike smiled as he thought back to the moment when he realized he was not alone.

Mike's coworker, Sue, was not really comfortable talking about what happened and asked if they could keep it just to themselves. Mike admits he was fine with that and just grateful to learn he was not losing his mind. The last frightening experience he had there was on a day they had a company carry-in meal. He was in the break room alone and opened his phone to take a picture of the spread. He snapped a few pics and went back to work. Later, when he was looking through the pictures, he nearly dropped his phone. In one of the pictures was a man. He was transparent but easy to make out as a white male with brown hair, wearing what looked like jeans and a dark shirt. He was standing in front of the counter where the food was, looking right at Mike. Mike was stunned. He knew it was impossible because he was the only one in the room at the time. The picture before it and right after it showed no one.

As he came to the end of sharing his haunted experience while working at the factory, Mike said,

I kick myself for never taking the picture off my old phone or emailing it to myself. Don't matter, though, because seeing that was validation for me. I showed it to Sue, and she actually began to shake and told me to put it away. It has been a long time since I worked there. I quit soon after the pictures were taken. Whenever I drive by, though, I wonder if that ghost or whatever it was it still there and how many other people have experienced what I did.

Dywer Instruments in Wolcott is still in operation and a benefit to the small community by providing jobs. There may never be an answer to who or what haunts the factory. It is fair to say, however, that as Mike shared, there are great people who have worked there over the years, and with that, many happy memories have been imprinted on the environment.

ABOUT THE AUTHORS

Dorothy Salvo Benson has written several books about the paranormal, also using the pen names Dorothy Salvo Davis and Maria Salvo. She developed her interest in the paranormal early on and, along with her passion for history, found a calling to validate others and their experiences. By connecting past events to current-day paranormal occurrences, she hopes to provide relief and assurance to those who are struggling to find answers and questioning their own sanity. Mrs. Salvo Benson grew up in South Florida in a Catholic Sicilian home. She felt fortunate to grow up in a melting pot of culture and diversity, experiencing many views on and perceptions of the paranormal. She relocated to Indiana, where today she is a teacher with a master's in education.

W.C. Madden learned how to write courtesy of the U.S. Air Force. He became a journalist in the military and achieved many awards before retiring in 1986 after a twenty-year career. Then he received his bachelor's degree through the GI Bill. He wrote his first book while still in the Air Force and has now authored forty-three of them. Many of those books have been published by The History Press and Arcadia Publishing. For the last decade, he has been the editor of *Monticello Magazine*.

Visit us at
www.historypress.com